Sites of Translation

SWEETLAND DIGITAL RHETORIC COLLABORATIVE

Series Editors:
Anne Ruggles Gere, University of Michigan
Naomi Silver, University of Michigan

————————————

The Sweetland Digital Rhetoric Collaborative Book Series publishes texts that investigate the multiliteracies of digitally mediated spaces both within academia as well as other contexts.

————————————

Sites of Translation: What Multilinguals Can Teach Us about Digital Writing and Rhetoric
    Laura Gonzales

Digital Samaritans: Rhetorical Delivery and Engagement in the Digital Humanities
    Jim Ridolfo

Rhizcomics: Rhetoric, Technology, and New Media Composition
    Jason Helms

Making Space: Writing, Instruction, Infrastrucure, and Multiliteracies
    James P. Purdy and Dànielle Nicole DeVoss, Editors

DIGITALCULTUReBOOKS, an imprint of the University of Michigan Press, is dedicated to publishing work in new media studies and the emerging field of digital humanities.

Sites of Translation

What Multilinguals Can Teach Us about Digital Writing and Rhetoric

Laura Gonzales

University of Michigan Press • Ann Arbor

Published in the United States of America by the
University of Michigan Press
Printed and bound by CPI Group (UK) Ltd, Croydon, CR0 4YY
First published September 2018

A CIP catalog record for this book is available from the British Library.

Library of Congress Cataloging-in-Publication Data

Names: Gonzales, Laura, author
Title: Sites of translation : what multilinguals can teach us about digital writing and
    rhetoric / Laura Gonzales.
Description: Ann Arbor : University of Michigan Press, 2018. | Series: Digital Rhetoric
    Collaborative | Includes bibliographical references and index. |
Identifiers: LCCN 2018014318 (print) | LCCN 2018032103 (ebook) | ISBN 9780472124343
    (e-book) | ISBN 9780472074037 (hardcover : alk. paper) | ISBN 9780472054039 (pbk.
    : alk. paper)
Subjects: LCSH: Translating and interpreting. | Translanguaging (Linguistics) |
    Multilingual communication. | Language and culture.
Classification: LCC P306 (ebook) | LCC P306 .G64   2018 (print) |
    DDC 418/.02—dc23
LC record available at https://lccn.loc.gov/2018014318

https://doi.org/10.3998/mpub.9952377

Cover illustration courtesy of Alexis Ruiz, owner of Printmeikiando in El Paso, TX.

The publisher gratefully acknowledges the support of the Sweetland Center for Writing in
making this book possible.

To my Gramps and para toda mi familia hermosa:
"It's family, it's family, it's family. I always believed in family."

Acknowledgments

I vividly remember a moment of looking up from my desk while packing my things following the conclusion of the first class period during my second semester of teaching writing. As may be common for many such "syllabus days," I had spent the previous seventy-five minutes telling my students what they might find in my class: high expectations, a lot of work, and hopefully an equal (if not greater) amount of learning. As a Latina professor in my early twenties during the first year of my master's program, I had already developed strategies for establishing my authority in classes, presumably so that students would take me and the course "seriously." I thought I had done a good job of discussing my expectations and the scaffolding of the course, one in which we were to, as I prophetically told my students, "study the discipline of writing studies while also practicing writing."

I will never forget looking up in that moment to have my eyes lock with the big, bright, green, fearful eyes of one of my students. Our eyes locked as tears ran down her face. In less than one minute, every shred of performative confidence left me as my heart ached, thumping as though it was trying to escape my body. In that moment, any pedagogical or professional training went out the window, as I walked over to my student and asked if we could step outside and talk.

"Hey, I'm sorry for pulling you aside. I just want to know if you're okay. Can I do anything to help?"

"No, miss. I'm sorry for crying. I just . . . I'm scared. Your class seems fun but also hard, and I'm just not good at this. We just got here from Colombia with my family last year, and since then, every time I write something, I get told that my English isn't good enough and that I'm going to fail at school. I just like you and don't want to fail. I just don't want you to think I don't care or I'm not trying. I'm trying. I will try."

I do not remember what I said in response to my student's comment, although I am sure it was not very useful. All I know is that in that moment, I promised myself that I would try too—try to connect with my students and to establish a classroom space guided by love and not fear, a space where "being good at English" is not the determining factor of success or the metric for measuring effort and intellect. Because of my students, I am still trying.

This book is for Camila and for the students who continue to make my job worth it. My students shape not only my teaching and my research but also how I view myself and my role in the world. I came into my research because I saw myself in my students. For that, I will be forever grateful.

I would be remiss to thank my students without also thanking the people who taught me how to teach, particularly how to teach with my heart and my mind in close relation. My MA advisory committee and mentors in the Department of Writing and Rhetoric at UCF—Elizabeth Wardle, Blake Scott, Martha Brenckle, Melody Bowdon, and Angela Rounsaville—continue to be the foundation on which I ground my career. Thank you all for bringing me into academia with the kindest guidance and with expectations that I now understand to be set only as high as what you saw in my potential.

The work in this book would also not have been possible without the guidance of my mentors at the Writing, Information, and Digital Experiences (WIDE) Research Center, where I learned to thread my love for language and teaching with my growing interests in technology and professional communication. I am incredibly grateful to Stuart Blythe for introducing me to the field of technical communication. His mentoring and continued support and his offer to nominate me for the Council for Programs in Technical and Scientific Communication Diversity Scholarship completely transformed my approach to research. Thank you, Stuart, for always being willing to listen to my ideas with the utmost attention and generosity, particularly when it came to the ideas that eventually shaped the methods I used in my work for this book. Thank you for sticking up for me and my ideas in more ways than I know.

To incredible friend, mentor, and light in the world Angela Haas, thank you for being the greatest role model I could ever imagine. Your continued encouragement and undying support for my success, happiness, and heart continue to fuel the work that I do within and way beyond this project. Your trust in me and my potential have shaped who I am as a researcher, teacher, and human being, and I continue to grow increasingly grateful for all that you do to support scholars of color in every corner of academia. You are the fire that keeps us all fighting and growing.

To my dissertation advisor and advocate, pillar of strength, and collaborator, Liza Potts, thank you for welcoming me into your family in more ways than one. Your fierce work as an advocate for my success led me to believe that I could write a book that matters in the world, one that would have influence in areas I never would have considered without your guidance. I am convinced that I would not have made it through graduate school (much less through this project) without your unending commitment to my success and my happiness. I know that supporting my decisions was not always easy, and I thank you for trusting me and teaching me to trust in myself.

I owe a tremendous amount of credit to the many mentors during and after my graduate study who guided me throughout the work reflected in this project, including Estrella Torrez, April Baker-Bell, Steven Fraiberg, Dànielle Nicole DeVoss, Julie Lindquist, and Jeff Grabill. Your continued guidance and support at several stages throughout this project gave me invaluable confidence and motivation.

I am also lucky to work within and across fields filled with people who taught me to fight for justice: Dr. Elaine Richardson, Gabi Ríos, Rebecca Zantjer, Steven Alvarez, Sara P. Alvarez, Tracey Flores, Michelle Eble, Anis Bawarshi, Susan Golab, Tatiana Batova, Emma Rose, Michele Simmons, Isidore Dorpenyo, Kristen Moore, Rebecca Walton, Natasha Jones, Esther Milu, Donnie Sackey, Becca Hayes, Casey Miles, Matt Gomes, Esme Murdock, Suban Nur Cooley, McKinley Green, Cristina Sánchez Martín, Aja Martinez, Janine Butler, Joy Robinson, Consuelo Salas, and Tetyana Zhyvotovska. Thank you for your continued generosity, friendship, and mentorship.

I am incredibly indebted to Naomi Silver, Anne Ruggles Gere, and the generous people at the Sweetland Digital Rhetoric Collaborative (DRC) and at the University of Michigan. From selecting me to be a DRC fellow, to connecting me with scholars across the country as I developed my line of research, to guiding the entire publication process of this manuscript, you have immensely influenced my career in more ways than I can count. Thank you for meeting with me, inspiring me, and, perhaps most important, believing in me and my work from the beginning. I am also grateful to the DRC Board for selecting my project for the DRC Book Prize and for providing invaluable feedback on this manuscript. Likewise, I want to recognize the tremendous work of DRC fellows Kristin Ravel and Brandy Dieterle and of Simone Sessolo at the Sweetland Center for Writing. Your in-depth feedback on earlier versions of this book shaped the direction of the project and my confidence in completing it. Thank you.

Thanks go to my dear friend and mentor Stacey Pigg, for nominating me to be a DRC fellow before I even entered my PhD program and for always believing in, supporting, and inspiring my work. I thank Jim Ridolfo for sharing his book proposal materials and encouraging me to pursue this project. Additional thanks go to Mary Francis, Sarah Dougherty, the team at the University of Michigan Press, and my blind reviewers, for strengthening this project through your support, guidance, and continued motivation.

The work reflected in this project would not have been possible without the immense generosity and leadership of Katie Coronado and the students at Knightly Latino News at UCF. Katie, thank you for dreaming with me and for bringing me into your Knightly Latino family. You are a true activist and advocate for the power of Latinx communities across the world, and I am so lucky to call you a collaborator and a friend. *Te agradezco por ser no solo mi colaboradora, pero sobre todo, mi amiga querida.* I also thank the amazing Brigitte Snedeker, for her continued involvement and trust in this project. Brigette, my pride in you and your amazing work continues to grow each day.

To my *familia* at the Language Services Department at the Hispanic Center of Western Michigan—Sara Proaño, Eloy Baez, Holly Rea, Carla Sanchez, Jaylynn Iff, and Maria Meneses—and to all the amazing interpreters and translators that I had the true privilege of working with on this project, thank you for wholeheartedly changing my life and my career. Sara, thank you for showing me how to be a leader who guides with her heart first. Thank you for welcoming me to your department, investing in my success, and making sure I never went a day without lunch =]. I love you and am consistently inspired by you.

As I was connecting with my community partners and building the work that eventually became this book, I was also learning about community building through the wonderful mentorship of the Cultivating New Voices among Scholars of Color (CNV) program, sponsored by the National Council of Teachers of English (NCTE). Thanks to the encouragement of April Baker-Bell and Juan Guerra, I was welcomed into the CNV community, where I got to connect with an invaluable network of scholars of color, who inspired and shaped this work. I am particularly grateful to my CNV cohort and to my CNV mentor Michelle Hall Kells, who told me early in this process that I could not send off my book manuscript until I was wholeheartedly proud of my work.

I thank the multiple organizations and groups of scholars who mentored me throughout this project: my community at the Computers and

Writing Conference, including Kristin Arola and Cheryl Ball, for their work supporting me and my colleagues through the Gail E. Hawisher and Cynthia L. Selfe Caring for the Future Award; Angela Haas, Janice Walker, and the generous community at the C&W Graduate Research Network; the Diversity Committee of the Council for Programs in Technical and Scientific Communication; the generous executive committee, driven by social justice, at the Association for Teachers of Technical Writing; the organizers and supporters of the Microsoft Research Student Competition at the Special Interest Group for the Design of Communication (SIGDOC); the amazing steering committee and community that is Women in Technical Communication; the NCTE/CCCC (Conference on College Composition and Communication) Latinx Caucus and members of the Scholars for the Dream community; and my family at the Smitherman/Villanueva Writing Retreat for Scholars of Color, generously created and supported by Adam Banks and his colleagues at Stanford University. Thank you for being the foundation and strength on which I built this project, through your feedback and guidance. I am eager to continue paying it forward in your name.

My academic boo and true sister Ann Shivers-McNair, you already know this book would not have happened without you. You have single-handedly secured my career and my happiness in more ways than one. I only grow increasingly excited for all the amazing things we will continue to do together. From the Writing Center couch to our super department, the future continues to look brighter because of you and our friendship. Words cannot express the impact you have had in my career and in my life.

Rachel Bloom-Pojar, *amiga del alma, mil gracias* for sharing a brain with me and for your careful and thoughtful read of this manuscript. Your encouragement, support, and friendship deeply influenced this project and, just as important, the success of my first year on the tenure track. Thank you for encouraging me to continue working with interpreters and for welcoming me to join you in your important work within the Rhetoric of Health and Medicine community. I am so excited to continue sharing space, ideas, and laughter with you.

It is rare to find someone who is incredibly talented and brilliant and also generous beyond words. I am lucky to have found that combination in the amazing Heather Noel Turner. Heather, thank you for investing your talent and time in designing all the illustrations depicted in this book and for investing your heart in supporting me throughout this process. Anyone who comes into contact with you is strengthened, and I am lucky to continue benefiting from your vigor, both as a research partner forever and as part of my family. A thank-you does not even begin to cover my debt to you, so I will keep trying to pay your tab at Forever XXI.

Ronisha Browdy, you probably do not even remember that you were the first one to visit the Hispanic Center with me, on a cloudy afternoon when we were desperately trying to find something good to eat in Michigan. You are the rock that carried us through graduate school and that continues to ground me through every struggle. Thank you, my boo, for your power and strength, your friendship and red roo.

The creative and technical elements of this book would not have come to fruition without the help of Gina Lawrence, Alexis Ruiz (owner of Printmeikiando), and the amazingly creative talents and constant inspiration from the power team of Ronnie Dukes and Elvira Carrizal-Dukes. Thank you, fam, for making this happen and for investing your talents in our collective vision. I am also immensely indebted to the army of support that I have been lucky enough to find at the University of Texas at El Paso as I completed the work of this project. Lucía Durá, thank you for being my writing partner and for encouraging me and reading my work. I value your friendship and your guidance immensely, and I thank you for all you have done to welcome me as a colleague and a friend.

Jen Clifton, Elenore Long, and Liz Kimball, our conversations about language and community work have been immensely helpful in motivating me to finish writing this book and to continue believing in the power of this project. Thank you for allowing me to join your family and for providing a space where ideas and friendship guide research and practice. I am lucky to have you in my life.

I thank Victor Del Hierro for singing *rancheras* with me at the top of our lungs through the streets of Lansing, teaching me about rhetoric, making sure I had enough fuel in my body to sustain my overwhelming schedule, loving me wholeheartedly and unconditionally, and being the foundation of everything good that I do in the world. *Te amo, lindo.* I am proud of the life that we have built and continue to build together.

I also thank *mi familia* Del Hierro for welcoming me to your family and to El Paso. Thank you for accepting, supporting, and loving me from the beginning and for taking care of me when I needed it most.

Finally, I thank the people who believed I could write a book before I even knew how to read. My *tía* Gigliola Roca, my *tío* Cristian Joffre, and my *primitas* Nadia, Bianca, and Juliana Joffre, *son mi inspiración por siempre.*

To my Tia Lizzie, thank you for believing in this *pitufina* and for being the pillar of strength to our whole family. I love you and my babies Sam and Amelia.

To my *mami*, my daddy buddy, my Zuli, and, most especially, my baby brother, Bert, everything I am is because of you. Thank you for teaching me to love deeply and fully and to invest myself completely toward finding happiness. You are my world.

•   Portions of chapter 6 were first published in Laura Gonzales and Heather Noel Turner, "Technical Communication, Translation, and Design at a Non-Profit Organization," *Technical Communication* 64, no. 2 (2017): 126–40, and in Laura Gonzales, "Using ELAN Video Coding Software to Analyze the Rhetorics of Translation," *Kairos: A Journal of Rhetoric, Technology, and Pedagogy* 21, no. 2 (2017), http://praxis.technorhetoric.net/tiki-index.php?page=PraxisWiki:_:ELAN

Contents

Introduction

"It's at the tip of my tongue!"
"Como se dice . . . ?"
"How do you say . . . ?"
"It's kind of like . . ."
"I almost had it!"
"It'll come back to me."
"I'm sorry. I don't speak Spanish."
"Disculpa, pero no hablo Inglés."
"Can you repeat, please?"

What do you do when you are trying to be understood—when you have your vision, your ideas, your thoughts so clearly available in your mind, yet this clarity ceases to exist as you try to communicate with others? What do you do to explain what you're thinking, when words are unavailable or perhaps unnecessary? This book is an attempt to illustrate what happens in these moments of communicative dissonance, when individuals make decisions about how to best share their ideas (or those of others) in a particular named language,[1] with specific audiences.

Certainly, I would argue that all human beings, regardless (and inclusive) of their linguistic backgrounds, have encountered moments like these in several contexts, working across linguistic and cultural differences to find common ground and understanding. Perhaps these moments come up on a trip to a location where people speak languages different than the ones we are accustomed to at home. We might struggle when attempting to ask someone for directions, feeling lost and insecure in an unfamiliar place. In these moments, we might approach someone for help, knowing that we do not speak the same languages, but hoping that we might find some way to communicate despite our linguistic differences. We might draw a picture, pull up a map on our phones, or use our bodies to point or gesture, working with another person to negotiate meaning outside the limitations of a single named language (e.g., Spanish, English).

I call these periods of communicative negotiation "translation moments"—instances in time when individuals pause to make a rhetorical decision about how to translate a word or phrase from one named language to another (Gonzales and Zantjer). Translation moments do not reference the entire process of translation. Instead, translation moments are those instances when we pause to ask, Should I use this word or that word? What word or phrase would be most appropriate in this context, for this audience? Should I use a word at all, or would a picture be more useful? Signaled by a pause, translation moments are instances of rhetorical action embedded in the process of language transformation.

We all know what it feels like to be misunderstood, and all types of misunderstanding are valid and worthy of study. Individuals who speak multiple languages—more specifically for this project, individuals in the United States who identify their heritage languages as something other than English mitigate communicative negotiations through experiences that can be of particular value to interdisciplinary language research and pedagogies. As Lachman Mulchand Khubchandani suggested, when multilinguals "cannot rely on a shared language or grammatical norms, they align participants, contexts, objects, and diverse semiotic cues to generate meaning" (31). This aligning of resources is where individuals leverage their full repertoires of communication (Frost and Blum Malley; Hawisher and Selfe). If multilinguals cannot rely on words to convey an idea in a specific language, we are motivated to creatively come up with other solutions, using any available modality to make our thoughts heard and understood outside the boundaries of standardized language systems (Gonzales, "Multimodality"; Ríos, "Cultivating," "Performing").

The term I use in this book to refer to individuals who have experiences navigating among and through multiple named languages is *multilinguals*, rather than *multilingual communicators* or other disciplinary terms, because the practice of working beyond standardized communicative norms is an embodied reality that extends to the core of individuals' humanity; multilingualism is not practiced through communication alone. Rather, multilinguals, specifically the individuals presented in this project, live in the flux of communicative difference both internally and externally, as they navigate linguistic movements alongside their identities, experiences, and aspirations, carrying difference in their words and in their bodies. Thus, to study the work of multilinguals, it is important to embrace a framework that accounts for multiple layers of analysis, including but not limited to language. In addition, to understand the experiences of multilinguals, I focus my analysis of translation on technical documents, live conversations, and situated genres that currently facilitate (or are influenced by) material activities (e.g., news stories, birth certificates, medical records). In this way, I aim to extend the important work that has been invested in studying literary translation and other creative genres, primarily by presenting frameworks that center on language transformations in technical and professional environments.

I introduce and embrace what I call "A Revised Rhetoric of Translation" as a framework for analyzing the translation work in this project. Countering traditional notions of translation that limit the analysis of language transformation to written alphabetic texts alone, A Revised Rhetoric of Translation is grounded in the notion that language is a culturally situated, embodied, lived performance. While the grammatical, technical, and alphabetic elements of translation continue to hold critical value, the embodied and cultural underpinnings of translation work are just as important. Hence, by sharing my analysis of translation moments through the framework of A Revised Rhetoric of Translation, I seek to "illuminate the highly distributed, embodied, translingual, and multimodal aspects of all communicative practice, something that is often overlooked or rendered invisible when analyzing final/finished texts, products, or performances" alone (Shipka, "Transmodality," 253). By recognizing and analyzing translation in written, multimodal, experienced, historical, and lived dimensions, I seek to draw attention to the embodied experiences and histories of multilinguals while also moving away from traditionally established dichotomies between material and immaterial elements and literacies (Ríos, "Performing"). Words and feelings do not exist independently; instead, they collectively form the experience of a multilingual's existence.

In many ways, I envision this project, my concept of "translation moments," and the framework of A Revised Rhetoric of Translation as contributions to emerging conversations regarding the mobility and fluidity of language in rhetoric and composition scholarship (Horner, Selfe, and Lockridge; Lu and Horner; Canagarajah). For decades, thanks largely to the work of scholars studying African American Language and English Education, researchers, teachers, and practitioners have been developing models to value and study the practices of students and professionals who communicate across languages in their daily interactions. For example, as early as 1974, when the Conference on College Composition and Communication (CCCC) was implementing the "Students' Right to Their Own Language" resolution to protect the use of "nonstandard" Englishes in college classrooms, researchers were discussing the importance of acknowledging students' movements across languages and the cultural and racial underpinnings of this work (Wolfram; Smitherman).

Since then, developments such as the 2013 NCTE "Definition of 21st Century Literacies" continue expanding rhetoric and composition's conceptions of standardized written English, advocating for "multiple, dynamic, and malleable" uses of language in and across classroom spaces (National Council of Teachers of English). Most recently, the "translingual turn" in composition also emerged to help rhetoric and composition scholars and teachers understand the fluidity of languages within their classrooms and programs. Translingualism rejects false binaries between "monolingual" and "multilingual" communication, arguing that all languages are constantly evolving and in motion and therefore that all language acts are inherently what was previously considered "multilingual." A translingual orientation rejects the idea of "monolingualism" and pushes for a shared understanding of all languaging (García and Li Wei) practices as emergent and polyvocal. These practices include the use of words across multiple language systems as well as the use of other semiotic practices, all of which work together to produce meaning. In turn, scholars working in translingualism make connections to conversations about multimodality in writing and writing instruction, arguing for a deeper understanding of how communication inherently functions outside perceived boundaries between languages, modalities, and media (Horner, Selfe, and Lockridge; Shipka, "Transmodality").

The field of rhetoric and composition continues making important arguments for the value of language fluidity, understanding that English, like all languages, is constantly in translation (Pennycook). Some researchers have also cautioned against the tendency to conflate inherent difference with homogeneity. Just because we understand all discourse as polyvocal and multiplicitous, we should not assume that language and languaging (García and Li Wei) acts are different, complex, and valuable in the same ways and to similar degrees. As Keith Gilyard reminds us in his recent critique of translingualism, "We all differ as language users from each other and in relation to a perceived standard. Often elided, however, is the recognition that we don't all differ from said standards in the same way. Given that context matters, a concept that is a key component of translingualism, one would always want to be careful not to level difference this way" (286). Because language is always connected to power, history, and ideology, it is important to recognize that language diversity is tied to differences in our lived experiences, in our access to and benefits from privilege, and in our cultural and racial backgrounds. To speak ethically of language fluidity, then, requires us to acknowledge the rhetorical and historical contexts in which this fluidity happens.

I present A Revised Rhetoric of Translation as a culturally situated orientation to studying linguistic fluidity, one that intentionally situates language work within broader systems of power, privilege, and oppression. Within the macrolevel framework of A Revised Rhetoric of Translation, I present translation moments as microlevel analytical units that can help researchers, teachers, and practitioners more clearly account for degrees and ranges of difference in language negotiation. Extending theoretical frameworks from which to conceptualize and protect language difference at the level of policy (e.g., CCCC's "Students' Right to Their Own Language," NCTE's "Definition of 21st Century Literacies"), translation moments are intended to guide studies on language difference at a level of practice (Guerra, *Language*). Thanks to previous work on language policies in rhetoric and composition and in related fields, I am lucky enough to come into my work with an understanding that all language is fluid, that language diversity is a reality in contemporary classrooms and workplaces, and that individuals' linguistic histories are critical and essential components of the "knowledge work" (Grabill) that communities create together—knowledge work that now increasingly encompasses the use of media and digital technologies in multiple languages (Barton and Lee) and that should continue to honor the intellectual labor of communities outside academia (Leon; Ríos, "Cultivating").

Stemming from this orientation to language diversity, I present the concept of "translation moments" as a way to better understand how language fluidity is enacted in professional and academic contexts and how the histories, lived experiences, and rhetorical abilities of all communicators are situated and deployed through their cultural languaging practices (García and Li Wei). By studying what communicators do during translation moments (i.e., how they make rhetorical decisions across languages and media, how they choose to leverage language repertoires in specific contexts), researchers, teachers, and practitioners can continue expanding their notions of writing beyond static, alphabetic, English-dominant texts. My goal here is to help rhetoric and composition, technical communication, and related fields continue expanding from the acknowledgment of language difference to a thorough understanding of what this difference entails, continuing to move us a way from blanket statements about the fluidity of language to a clear understanding of the consequences and exigencies for our linguistic movements. In particular, I am interested not just in showing that language difference exists but also in clearly and visually illustrating how language difference is negotiated and what these negotiations can contribute to the research and teaching of writing across languages, communities, and platforms.

There are numerous frameworks for researching language fluidity, from a wide range of disciplines and fields: for example, translanguaging (García and Li Wei), translingualism (Horner, Lu, et al.), and codemeshing/codemashing (Fraiberg; Young and Martinez). Here, I focus specifically on translation, due to the practical nature and the history of this practice and profession. While much of the research on language in rhetoric and composition is situated or placed in relation to classroom settings, my goal in this study is to further understand language fluidity in professional contexts, thus gaining a broader understanding of what and how language diversity contributes to contemporary classrooms and professional spaces. In developing my concept of "translation moments," I want to honor the rhetorical labor enacted through language transformations both in and outside the classroom, emphasizing how the impetus and exigency for translation directly impact the processes and products of this work.

When multilinguals translate, they are transforming language to make information accessible, for themselves and/or for others. Translators, particularly in professional and technical settings, cannot get infinitely bogged down in the ideological or theoretical underpinnings of their work. Instead, translators, particularly the translators depicted in this project, often have to make immediate, high-stakes decisions about how to transform information in the moment—as they translate an urgent medical or technical document, as they interpret for a health practitioner during a birth, or as they interpret a community event with hundreds of attendees. Analyzing the practices of translation in these moments can help researchers and practitioners understand what language fluidity entails—the decisions, the resources, the modalities, and the practices embedded in what is traditionally perceived as a simple, "once and done" process of language transformation (Gonzales and Zantjer).

I ground the research that fuels this book in two seemingly simple questions:

1. What do communicators do as they translate information across languages?
2. What digital and material tools and rhetorical strategies do communicators use when translations are not immediately available (i.e., during translation moments)?

By researching these questions with community organizations, I have come to understand that the rhetoric embedded in multilingual communication requires the negotiation and purposeful layering of communicative strategies. These strategies include the use of verbal and written words, as well as the movement of ideas through other modalities, such as visuals and digitally mediated technologies. Through my work with multilinguals, I realized that language negotiation, particularly the adaptation of languages in situated community and professional contexts, requires translators to live and relive instances of communicative negotiation, making decisions in the moment based on our previous experiences with language, power, and marginalization. These decisions and the rhetoric that guides these situated practices can help further unpack the contributions and significance of linguistic diversity, both in and outside of writing classrooms.

Rather than working from strictly theoretical frameworks regarding language diversity, I herein highlight how and why multilinguals coordinate semiotic resources as they translate information for specific purposes in specific moments in time. In chapter 1, I further introduce my concept of "translation moments," situating multilingual communication in the experiences of translators who navigate communication across modes and languages for their specific communities. I discuss my own orientation to and experiences with translation, and I present the concept of "translation moments" as an analytical framework that takes into account emerging conversations in rhetoric and composition, sociolinguistics, and translation studies.

Understanding the rhetorical strategies enacted by multilingual communicators during translation moments requires the use of visual and digital methods that can provide intricate illustrations of linguistic movements. In chapter 2, I outline my research design for this project, describing how I incorporate participatory, community-driven visual/digital methods and methodologies to study translation across contexts. These methods draw from work in rhetoric and composition and in technical communication, thus accounting for both the academic and professional contexts in which translation is enacted. In chapter 3, I further describe translation as a multimodal activity that requires the constant negotiation of tools, technologies, and modalities. Like many contemporary forms of communication, translation (and multilingual communication more broadly) now increasingly takes place in digital contexts. In turn, as I demonstrate in chapter 3, translation is a multimodal practice that requires the combination, adaptation, and manipulation of multiple semiotic modes to convey meaning.

Centering linguistic difference in rhetoric and composition requires us to recognize translation in its cultural-rhetorical contexts. In chapter 4, I elaborate on the framework of A Revised Rhetoric of Translation, which I developed to further understand how language fluidity is grounded in the iterative work of multimodal/multilingual communicators. A Revised Rhetoric of Translation posits translation as a culturally situated (rather than neutral), cyclical (rather than linear), and creative (rather than mechanical) practice. This macrolevel orientation to language difference guides the presentation of data in this project.

Chapters 5 and 6 are the core case studies that inform the arguments I make in this book. In these chapters, I further illustrate A Revised Rhetoric of Translation, specifically as it is enacted by translators with various backgrounds and ranges of expertise in language negotiation. In chapter 5, I introduce the translation work that takes place at Knightly Latino News, a bilingual (Spanish and English) student-run organization in news broadcasting, located at the University of Central Florida (UCF) in Orlando. When I first started working with students at Knightly Latino News, this group was entirely volunteer-based, meaning that participants were volunteering to translate news stories published in English on the English-based network Knightly News into Spanish, to better serve the Latinx community in Orlando. Since then, thanks to the incredible work of their faculty leader, Katie Coronado, Knightly Latino News has grown into a course that fuels an ongoing Latino media initiative at UCF. In chapter 5, through the work of my generous student collaborators, I highlight how translation requires the savvy rhetorical negotiation of digital and nondigital modalities. In addition, I introduce the work of two student translators at Knightly Latino News, Natalie and Brigitte, who combine their cultural understanding of their languages and communities with their knowledge of digital translation algorithms to provide culturally situated Spanish translations for their community.

After working with student translators at Knightly Latino News, I was fortunate enough to connect with an organization of professional translators and interpreters who work in the Language Services Department at the Hispanic Center of Western Michigan. The Language Services Department is a small translation and interpretation business located within the bigger, nonprofit Hispanic Center. Led by their brilliant director, Sara Proaño, the Language Services Department employs over thirty Spanish-speaking and English-speaking translators and interpreters. In chapter 6, I illustrate how each of these employees brings specific cultural and technological capital into their workplace, creating a multilingual synergy that allows the organization to serve thousands of Spanish-speaking community members each year. Further, chapter 6 highlights how professional translators, through their experiences navigating languages, layer multimodalities that encompass the use of digital tools, writing skills, and embodied experiences. All of these components are critically important to successful multilingual, multimodal communication.

In chapter 7, I draw on the case studies presented in chapters 5 and 6 and argue that translation practices can be further embedded into writing research and instruction, providing frameworks (i.e., translation moments, A Revised Rhetoric of Translation) through which writers can both research and teach rhetorical dexterity. Moving away from deficit-based models often used to reference multilingual communication, chapter 7 positions linguistic diversity as an asset that should be further highlighted and valued in the training of students and professionals from all linguistic and cultural backgrounds. By further discussing the practical applications of the concept of "translation moments" and the framework of A Revised Rhetoric of Translation, this book's concluding chapter serves as an example and a call to develop further models to help researchers understand how language fluidity is enacted in various contexts, including but not limited to the classroom.

My ultimate goal in this book is to present approaches and lenses for studying language difference at a level of practice, illustrating how translation is leveraged as a rhetorical strategy by marginalized communities both in and outside the United States. As rhetoric and composition continues working to protect and value the communicative practices of all students and as technical communication scholars continue building frameworks for enacting social justice in professional spaces, it is important that we understand not only that language difference is present but also that the practice of language negotiation is directly situated and reflective of the work that individuals from the margins (Smitherman and Villanueva) have had to do to be heard in the United States, for many years. Thus, this project is merely an attempt to listen—and to help rhetoric and composition, technical communication, and related fields listen—to the motivations, the struggles, and, more important, the strengths that evolve from the practice of moving across communicative norms in order to be heard, acknowledged, and understood.

1 • Translation Moments as a Framework for Studying Language Fluidity

> Languages do not exist as real entities in the world and neither do they
> emerge from or represent real environments; they are, by contrast, the
> inventions of social, cultural, and political *movements*. (Makoni and
> Pennycook, 2)

Coming into Translation

I was born in Santa Cruz, Bolivia, the industrial hub of a plurinational[1]
country with over forty-two nationally recognized languages. As the business center of Bolivia, Santa Cruz is one of the few cities in the country
with semi-reliable Internet connectivity and global business potential. It is
the place where people from all over the country come to make money.

Each day, thousands of people enter the city of Santa Cruz to sell products or provide services. As a result, when walking through the streets of
this city, you will encounter several acts of translation, with over forty-two
languages interacting to set prices, discuss negotiations, and build connections. Often, shared words are not available or necessary in these transactions. Instead, people employ any available mode to communicate, using
their bodies, drawing figures, texting, singing, dancing, chirping, clapping,
whistling, twirling, laughing—all to help each other overcome complex
linguistic negotiations. In cases like these, translation is not just a classroom activity or a theoretical framework; it is a means for survival, as individuals rely on multilingual communication to sell products and make a
living. In these contexts, acts of translation are inherently multimodal activities, as people extend beyond alphabetic words to layer communicative
resources that might help them transform meaning beyond the limitations
of any language or alphabet.

Having witnessed acts of translation at various stages of my life and

Fig. 1. Business in the streets of Santa Cruz, Bolivia

having negotiated my own linguistic transitions as an immigrant in the United States, I know that multilingual communicators have developed cultural, rhetorical, and technical skills through their lived experiences and practice these skills as they transform information across languages. When multilinguals cannot immediately decide on an adequate word in a specific language, we make do with whatever resources are most appropriate and available. This, I argue, is where creativity and survival render multimodal/

multilingual communication, in the spaces where common words are hard to access.

To understand how individuals transform information across languages by using a wide range of semiotic resources and practices, I call for a focus on "translation moments"—instances in time when individuals pause to make a rhetorical decision about how to translate a specific word or phrase for a specific audience in a specific context. As I mention in this book's introduction, translation moments do not encompass the entire process of translation. Instead, translation moments are those instances when we pause and debate among several options to decide how a word, phrase, or idea would be represented best in a different language. To further illustrate here what I mean by translation moments, I will first share a brief anecdote from an early visit to one of my research sites. Using this anecdote as a grounding example, I will then discuss how translation moments can help researchers further understand the practices of linguistic fluidity in and outside the classroom.

Translation Moments in Practice: Sandra Translates *Mazorca*

After deciding that I wanted to study translation in a community organization, I began volunteering at local community events facilitated by and for Latinx community members. In particular, I was interested in seeing how we Spanish-speaking Latinx *gente* living in the United States leverage our resources (both material and linguistic) to help each other in *la lucha* of succeeding in English-dominant America. During this search, I volunteered to help with a Comprando Rico y Sano (Shopping Tasty and Healthy) event hosted by a local nonprofit organization in Grand Rapids, Michigan. Sponsored through a grant intended to promote healthy eating choices in the Latinx community, this event invited people from the area to learn more about healthy eating.

To help set up for this presentation, I was asked to lay out material—in both Spanish and English—to be made available for community members as they entered the venue. For example, on all tables set up for community members at the event, we laid out flyers titled *MyPlate* or *MiPlato*, illustrating portion sizes the sponsoring organization deemed to be adequate for dinner (see fig. 2).

As the presentation began, the health promoter (or *promotora*), Sandra, began sharing resources and discussing family eating habits for her community. Sandra presented information primarily in Spanish, though she used English when she thought it would be useful to help her audience

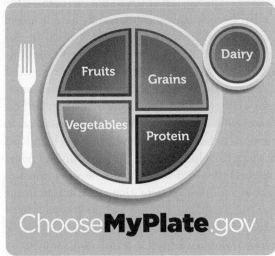

Fig. 2. Bilingual *My-Plate* flyers on food portions

understand her message. Sandra began her presentation by assuring her audience that although they all came from different places, she would do her best to make sure they could understand each other: "Yo creo que nos vamos a entender, aunque somos de differentes paises" (*I think we're going to understand each other, even though we all come from different countries*). Although all the participants in attendance identified as speakers of Spanish, Sandra understood that different Latin American countries use different Spanishes for different purposes and contexts. Hence, Sandra explained that she would do her best to contextualize information in Spanish to fit the conventions of participants from different South American and Central American countries.

As Sandra continued with her presentation, she paused when discussing corn on the cob as a potential healthy dinner option for the families in attendance. During this pause in her presentation, Sandra mentioned a previous presentation at which she used the Spanish word *mazorca* to describe corn on the cob. An audience member from Mexico who was at that previous presentation did not interpret *mazorca* to mean corn on the cob and instead thought Sandra's suggestion was that audience members serve dry corn to their families (which did not seem right to the audience member).

In this moment in the presentation I attended, Sandra informed her audience, "When I reference *mazorca*, I mean corn on the cob." Then she showed a picture of corn on the cob to further clarify what she meant when she used the word *mazorca*. She used the English phrase "corn on the cob" to further reference what her audience members may have heard in the past when referring to this food item, and she used a visual in this multimodal interaction, to provide added support for the clarification she was trying to make. Thus, Sandra's navigation of how to translate the word *mazorca* required a pause in her dialogue, followed by the rhetorical combination of words, an image, and several gestures as she made her clarifications. In this specific instance, Sandra layered several semiotic resources to translate and adapt information for her audience, leveraging her linguistic, cultural, and material resources to help her along the way. Sandra's pause in her discussion as she reached the word *mazorca*, followed by clarifications (e.g., telling a story about a previous presentation and using an image to show the audience what she meant by *mazorca*), encompassed what I came to define as a "translation moment." If I were analyzing this specific presentation for this project, I would identify a translation moment in Sandra's pause and would code the actions that followed as multimodal rhetorical strategies enacted by a translator during her translation process. In this specific instance, I would code Sandra as using storytelling, gesturing, and visuals as rhetorical strategies enacted to navigate this specific translation moment. Using the framework of A Revised Rhetoric of Translation, I would contextualize my coding of Sandra's translation strategies within the broader cultural context of the event being analyzed, working to unpack the motivations and histories of attendees at this event and of Sandra herself as the translator.

Following this initial translation moment, Sandra proceeded to pause at several points in her presentation and ask her audience how they defined specific words (e.g., "How do you say 'beans' to your kids?" and "How does your family describe grocery shopping?"), thus negotiating languages as she presented information to a multilingual, culturally diverse audience familiar with Spanishes and Englishes (and other languages) to various degrees. She situated the information she was presenting within the context of that specific audience during that specific presentation. The translation in this example required that the communicator, Sandra, not only find a literal replacement of words from one language to another but also situate these words to fit the specific cultural practices of her audience—what some technical communication practitioners call "localization" (Agboka; Sun). In this way, the translation required both the adaptation of words and the contextualization (i.e., localization) of ideas across languages, cultures, and modalities simultaneously.

Briefly Defining "A Revised Rhetoric of Translation"

In chapter 4, I further describe the framework of A Revised Rhetoric of Translation. Here, I find it important to clarify that my analysis of translation moments, while grounded in situated translation events (e.g., Sandra's discussion of *mazorca*), is also directly linked to broader cultural contexts and embodied experiences. A traditional rhetoric of translation might be defined as one that situates language work within visible, often alphabetic activities (i.e., the actual process of transforming information from a source language to a target language). This traditional rhetoric positions translation as the replacement of one word in one language with a similar word in another language, or an "attempt to duplicate meaning interlingually" (Batova and Clark, 223). Traditional definitions of translation assume that translators are simply information conduits who replace words across languages. However, recent work in technical communication and translation studies counters this perception of translation as a word-for-word replacement process (Agboka; Batova and Clark; Gonzales and Zantjer; Sun; Walton, Zraly, and Mugengana).

For example, the concept of localization is now frequently associated with translation in technical communication. Localization aims to address linguistic and cultural expectations of specific cultures in specific contexts (Batova and Clark, qtd. in Gonzales and Zantjer, 273), accounting "for not only the replacement of words, but also [the adaptation of] materials to convey overall meaning from one culture to another" (Gonzales and

Zantjer, 273). While the translation of a technical document might only entail the transformation of words from a source language to a target language, the localization of this document might encompass changes in images and visuals to meet the cultural expectations of users in the target language.

The concept of localization, through its focus on culture and usability, is a move away from a traditional rhetoric of translation. While localization is used primarily in technical communication and user experience, A Revised Rhetoric of Translation is an orientation to studying language transformation across disciplinary and professional/academic boundaries. A Revised Rhetoric of Translation is a framework for approaching the study of language transformation in both academic and professional spaces, one that allows researchers to situate translation moments within their cultural-rhetorical contexts. While traditional definitions of translation might focus on the transformation of words alone, localization might highlight the cultural adaptation and usability of information across cultures. A Revised Rhetoric of Translation allows researchers to account for the transformation of words and other modalities, the localization of cultural elements in written and multimodal artifacts, and the lived experiences, cultural histories, and current material realities of the translator(s) and target audience(s) engaged in these activities. I identify and unpack translation moments through this multi-layered orientation.

Defining "Translation Moments"

The specific translation moment illustrated through Sandra's discussion of *mazorca* is not an anomaly in the daily experiences of multilinguals. Indeed, communicators who move across named languages and cultures in their daily interactions often use multimodal resources (e.g., images, gestures, sounds) to convey their thoughts when specific words are not available or necessary. If we cannot immediately decide on a word to convey what we are thinking in a specific language, we will use other tools—our bodies, drawings, digital technologies, sounds—to get across our point. Thus, the rhetorical decisions that communicators make during translation moments are instances of multilingual, multimodal communication, illustrating the fluidity of languages beyond any standardized alphabetic systems. To define translation moments as interdisciplinary analytical frameworks, I draw on scholarship in sociolinguistics, rhetoric and composition, and translation studies.[2]

Defining "Translation Moments" through Sociolinguistics

Understanding translation moments requires us to acknowledge language as a living, fluid, constantly emerging practice. Since and before the early 1900s, linguists have challenged the structural perception of languages as discrete alphabetic entities, instead situating linguistic actions in the culturally bound ideologies and interactions of individuals (Gumperz and Hernandez). For decades, enunciated signs (i.e., words) have been conceived as always traversed by extralinguistic elements (Otheguy, García, and Reid). These elements include the actions of speakers, the context in which the utterances are being shared, and the cultural backgrounds and lived experiences of those engaging in the interaction. This dialogic theory posits that language "acquires life 'in concrete verbal communication, and not in the abstract linguistic system of language forms, not in the individual psyche of speakers'" (García and Li Wei, quoting Voloshinov, 6). Hence, language lives in and through human interaction and cannot be reduced to alphabetic structured categories that are extracted and transported from one context to another. Models for understanding translation across languages must also account for this fluidity, understanding that translation choices will change and adapt based on context and rhetorical situation.

Because language is always dependent on the context in which it is used, named language categories (e.g., Spanish, English, French) never reference one static set of codes. There are many Spanishes and Englishes constantly being developed, adapted, and repurposed in every interaction. As sociolinguists and educators Ofelia García and Li Wei explain, "English is regarded as a language only in comparison with the existence of other languages such as French, Spanish, or Chinese. None of these languages exist on their own, and all languages are in contact with others—being influenced by others, and containing structural elements from others" (406). Thus, when individuals who identify as bilingual or multilingual translate information, they are not moving across two or more sets of linguistic codes. All individuals draw on their entire semiotic repertoire in each interaction, identifying the utterances that are most appropriate for a specific audience in a specific context. If I identify as a speaker of Spanish and English, for example, I do not have two separate containers to draw on when I interact with a specific person. Instead, as psycholinguists and neuropsychologists have shown, individuals have one linguistic repertoire or container that they use in all interactions. As a person who identifies as a speaker of Spanish and English, I make decisions about which utterances to use when talking with another individual. Sometimes I use Spanish, sometimes I use English, and sometimes I use both (what García and Li Wei might call "translanguaging").

In addition, as I move across Spanish and English, I use my entire communicative repertoire to translate my ideas. Sometimes I translate using words alone, but I more often translate using words in combination with other objects, including but not limited to my body. When I translate, I use all my resources to make meaning, gauging the reactions of my audience and adapting my actions accordingly (Gonzales and Zantjer; Gumperz and Hernandez). In this way, the power of language fluidity lies not within bounded words and symbol systems but with the rhetorical expertise of the communicators negotiating meaning across contexts (Canagarajah). The point of analyzing translation from a rhetorical perspective (and through A Revised Rhetoric of Translation specifically) is not so much to gain an understanding of what words translators choose to use but, rather, to understand how, when, and why translators are choosing specific words or phrases in specific moments in time. For this reason, situating theories of linguistic mobility in an analysis of translation moments allows me to connect language transformations to their rhetorical contexts, understanding how the decisions that translators make are always influenced by both internal and external factors.

Defining "Translation Moments" in Rhetoric and Composition

In rhetoric and composition, theories like translingualism support the fluid, socially constructed notion of language established by sociolinguists (Li Wei; Vigouroux and Mufwene; Canagarajah). Through a translingual framework, languages are treated "'as always emergent, in process (a state of becoming), and their relations as mutually constitutive,' rather than 'as discrete, preexisting, stable, and enumerable entities'" (Gonzales, "Multimodality," quoting Lu and Horner, "Translingual Literacy," 587). A translingual orientation to rhetoric and composition, as presented by scholars like Lu and Horner, Canagarajah, and many others, envisions classrooms as what García and Li Wei call "translanguaging spaces," where students are encouraged to enact the full potential of their linguistic repertoires to make rhetorical arguments for various audiences. As defined by García and Li Wei, translanguaging spaces "allow multilingual individuals to integrate social practices (and thus 'language codes') that have been formerly practiced separately in different places" (508). Translanguaging spaces establish "a social space for the multilingual user by bringing together different dimensions of their personal history, experience and environment, their attitude, belief and ideology, their cognitive and physical capacity into one coordinated and meaningful performance" (Li Wei, 1223).

Li Wei's notion of translanguaging practices as "coordinated and meaningful performance[s]" is critical to my presentation and analysis of translation moments. Because language is a performance contextualized in the exigencies and affordances of specific rhetorical situations, it is important to acknowledge how our linguistic performances are influenced by extrinsic cultural and social factors. In the cases of sociolinguistics, education, and rhetoric and composition, theoretically acknowledging the translanguaging practices of students has been a long, ongoing battle for advocacy and justice in the establishment and recognition of classrooms as translanguaging spaces. In rhetoric and composition specifically, countless studies illustrate the important work being developed to establish and maintain language policies that honor our students' cultural and linguistic histories (e.g., Canagarajah; Young and Martinez). These studies have presented rhetoric and composition teachers and practitioners with useful frameworks (e.g., translingualism, translanguaging, code meshing, code switching) for theorizing language diversity in classrooms and community contexts.

Yet, as scholars like Juan Guerra argue, there is a difference between, on one hand, "policy issues" in regard to language use and, on the other hand, what he deems to be a "matter of practice" in language negotiation. Theories like translingualism, for example, provide a useful orientation to theorizing language difference, particularly in reference to the inherent linguistic diversity that is present and should be valued and protected in rhetoric and composition classrooms. In my discussion and use of translation moments, I aim to reference these theoretical orientations to language diversity (orientations that acknowledge the linguistic diversity present in all communicative contexts) to account for both language policy issues and matters of practice, material exigencies that take place on the ground as communicators navigate their linguistic repertoires to make meaning in specific moments in time; that is, I aim not only to acknowledge that language diversity is present in all communicative acts but also to understand how these linguistic transformations take place in specific rhetorical contexts. This is where translation studies and the profession of technical translation inform my understanding and presentation of translation moments.

Translation Moments in Practice: Perspectives from Translation Studies

Peter Newmark defines translation as "rendering the meaning of a text into another language in the way that the [author] intended [in] the [source] text" (5). Similarly, Müller defines translation as "the replacement of text in a source language by text in a target language equivalent in meaning" (207). The notion of linguistic "replacement" embedded in traditional definitions of translation echo the static conceptions of language embraced by early structural linguistics. However, while there are still some cases in which translation is perceived as a simple process of language replacement, Newmark clarifies that "translation cannot simply reproduce, or be, the original [source]" (76). Instead, all translations are products of broad rhetorical negotiations, which include factors like "the individual style or idiolect of the Source Text (SL) author," the "conventional grammatical and lexical usage" for a specific type of text, "content items referring to specific Source Text culture[s]," "the typical format of a text," and the "expectations of the readership" (Newmark, 5). Thus, in practice, translation reflects fluid, multimodal conceptions of language, positioning translators as the individuals who perform intellectual rhetorical work and coordination of semiotic practices as they make decisions about how information can be understood by audiences from various cultural and linguistic backgrounds.

The more recent "critical turn" in translation studies posits that "classic conceptualizations of translation do not fully capture its complexity and contextuality" (Yajima and Toyosaki, 93). Critical perspectives in translation studies position the work of translators as political, reflecting the cultural histories, lived experiences, and ideologies of the individuals who perform linguistic negotiations as they transform information across languages (Baker; Robinson; Tymoczko). Since translation "takes place in a specific social and historical context that informs and structures it," political and cultural forces always influence the decisions that translators make in the moment of translation (Jacquemond, 93, qtd. in Yajoma and Toyosaki, 91). As a translator adapts information across languages, the translator has to consider the perceived intentions of the author(s) of the source text, the linguistic and grammatical features of both a source language and a target language, the nature of the information being presented in the source text, and the potential dispositions to language encompassed in the envisioned audience for the translation.

In addition, because translation now frequently takes place in digital contexts, translators have to account for the digital and multimodal design elements embedded both in their source text and in their translated documents (Gonzales and Turner). Translators must understand how to replicate meaning across languages using alphabetic, visual, and digital elements, moving across platforms and languages simultaneously to accomplish their work. Throughout this process, a translator must also negotiate her or his own perceptions and positionality on the issue(s) being described in the source text, doing her or his best to successfully represent the intentions of the source text's author. In this way, contemporary translation practices are multilingual/multimodal activities that require extensive rhetorical negotiation. Translation moments, in turn, are analytical frameworks that can help rhetoric and composition researchers and technical communicators better understand how and when specific modes are deployed by multilingual communicators throughout the translation process. Thus, translation moments can inform how researchers, teachers, and practitioners understand language fluidity as a situated practice (rather than only as an ideological orientation or policy).

Figure 3 illustrates how translation moments fit into what might be considered a typical translation workflow in a professional context (Dimitrova; Gonzales and Turner).[3] In the diagram, the "input" segment on the right-hand side represents the beginning of the process, where a client submits an initial translation project or when a translator first opens a document to translate. The "output" segment on the left-hand side represents when the translation has to be delivered, returned to a client, or published in a particular venue. Thus, figure 3 emphasizes that translators are typically working with the understanding that they will have to deliver a translated product based on a predetermined timeline; there is always an exigency and expectation for translation work, pushing professional translators to make informed rhetorical decisions for particular audiences in specific moments in time.

In addition to the submission and delivery periods, figure 3 illustrates other common activities encompassed in the translation process: reading, research, language transformation, design, formatting, editing, proofreading, and collaborating. Although every translator's process is slightly different (Dimitrova), the activities labeled in figure 3 are common practices in the written translation workflow (Gonzales and Turner). For instance, following the initial submission of a translation project, the translator may do some preliminary reading of the document to assess the type of language or project encountered. Next, the translator might do some research on the topics being covered in the document being translated, aiming to understand the subject area that the translator will be working within for this project. After getting a better sense of the

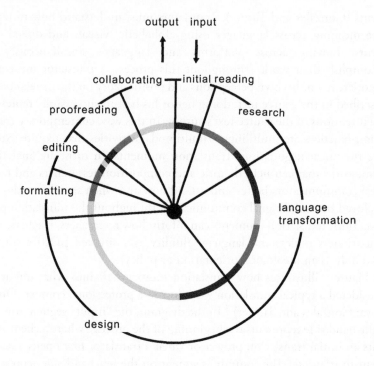

Fig. 3. Representative translation process with translation moments

subject area at hand, the translator might begin actually transforming words on the document itself. Then, the translator may engage in some design activities while transforming visual information on the translated document. Throughout this process, the translator may also engage in formatting, editing, and proofreading activities and may even collaborate with other translators, to share ideas or garner stories to help with decision making in the translation process, before delivering the final product. Thus, the gray text and gray segmented lines in figure 3 represent activities that may be experienced at different lengths and to different degrees, depending on the context of the translation and the specific experiences and common practices of a translator.

Although the solid gray lines in figure 3 represent discreet translation activities within the translation process, the multi-shaded lines in the diagram represent translation moments. As evidenced by the varying lengths of the multi-shaded segments in figure 3, translation moments are not consistent across the entire process of translation. Instead, translation moments are instances of rhetorical negotiation that can take place at different points throughout the translation process, as translators pause to decide which word to use for a particular audience, which sentence phrasing would be most effective in a particular context, and how to best convey a specific idea in a particular language. Much like pauses in the writing process, translation moments are instances where translators pause to think and decide how to transform a specific word, phrase, or concept.

As evidenced by the varying lengths of the multi-shaded line segments in figure 3, translation moments can vary in frequency and duration, depending, once again, on the context of the translation project and on the specific experiences and practices of the translator. Translation moments can take place during any other activity in the translation process (e.g., during research, design, or formatting), as translators pause to make decisions within their process. Translation moments can also extend between activities—for example, as translators move between editing and design in order to make a specific decision about how to transform a word or phrase from one language to another. Hence, a translator may experience several translation moments during a translation process, pausing as needed to define and transform a specific term, word, or concept.

During these pauses (i.e., translation moments), translators may use a wide range of different strategies (e.g., Sandra's layering of a visual with various gestures) to contextualize translations for their particular audience. These strategies include the use of words in both source and target languages (e.g., Spanish and English), but they may also encompass the use of other semiotic resources and practices, such as visuals, gesturing, and storytelling. Thus, translation moments are the instances where multilingual communicators are pushed to think beyond the limitations of alphabetic languages and symbol systems, using any mode or resource available to make meaning (e.g., using Google Translate, gesturing and telling stories with another translator, or drawing or sketching a description for a concept that may not have a specific name in a given language). For this reason, as I discuss further in chapters 2 and 3, translation moments represent the rhetorical invention embedded in the translation process, signaling a space where translators employ multilingual, multimodal resources to make information available across languages. Although we can understand all language as fluid and constantly in motion, situating this fluidity within the work of translators and, more specifically, within translation moments can help researchers more intricately understand how, when, and why multilingual communicators layer communicative practices and semiotic resources to make information available across languages. Following this understanding of what translation moments are and how they fit into the more general activities of translation, chapters 2 through 6 of this study move on to describe the various strategies and practices performed by translators during translation moments and to make a broader argument for the value of translation in the research and pedagogies of rhetoric and composition and of technical communication.

• Drawing on my work with the communities described in this project and on my own experiences as a translator, I understand that translators do not pull from distinct, static sets of linguistic containers (e.g., labeled "Spanish" or "English") in any given interaction. Based on the same experiences, I also understand that any translation interaction requires translators to present a "final" version of their linguistic conversions, whether through written translated documents or through live verbal translations of information (what practitioners call "interpretation"). Hence, I situate the studies presented in this project within the work of translators because of the very exigency embedded in this profession, because of the need to provide a translation "answer," even if this answer changes in each utterance within any given context.

As I will further discuss in the case studies presented in chapters 5 and 6, translation moments extend theories of language in rhetoric and composition (e.g., Canagarajah; Horner, Lu, et al.), sociolinguistics (e.g., García and Li Wei), and critical translation studies (e.g., Yajima and Toyosaki), situating language fluidity in the multilingual, multimodal communicative practices of contemporary writers and professionals. Translation moments are analytical units that may be coded within the translation processes of multilingual communicators, providing a framework for studying the process and practice of translation rather than solely focusing on the products of these negotiations. Perhaps more important, translation moments are inherently multimodal and multilingual, reflecting the lived experiences of multilingual communicators who constantly think across languages, modalities, and technologies, to transform and adapt information for various audiences.

In translation studies, researchers have begun to pay attention to how translators leverage multimodal resources when translating information, acknowledging the role that visuals and other non-alphabetic resources play in the communication of ideas across languages (Ketola). In rhetoric and composition, researchers have also recently begun to acknowledge multimodal resources as part of the translingual orientation to writing, emphasizing how digital and non-alphabetic tools and technologies can be used to communicate ideas beyond the limitations of standard written English (Canagarajah; Lu and Horner). By embedding translation moments within these conversations, coding specifically for how multimodal resources are leveraged during translation processes, I position translation as a multimodal activity that can further impact how we recognize and respond to language difference in both professional and academic spaces. To this end, in chapter 2, I further explain how I studied translation moments, such as Sandra's discussion of *mazorca*, to better understand how individuals layer multimodal resources to translate information rhetorically. In addition, I there further contextualize my study of translation moments in my relationships with the translators who make this work happen, arguing that to fully understand and acknowledge the work of translation, scholars and teachers need to make increasing efforts to understand the cross-cultural, multilingual lived experiences of linguistically diverse individuals.

2 • Research Design

As I describe in chapter 1, I chose to use translation moments as my primary unit of analysis in this project, in an attempt to ground conversations about language fluidity in the lived practices and experiences of multilinguals. When I analyze translation moments, I consider language not only from the perspective of language theories and policies but also from an orientation of practice and situated performance, paying attention to how and when multilinguals make specific rhetorical choices in their interactions. Further, I theorize and analyze translation moments through multimodal frameworks that consider not only linguistic or alphabetic negotiations but also embodied, material, and digital practices that are embedded in contemporary communication (Haas; Ríos). In this way, I aim to bridge research in multimodality with work that advocates for the value of linguistic diversity in and outside of writing classrooms (Bowen and Whithaus; Canagarajah; Guerra; Fraiberg).

By blending multilingual/multimodal frameworks for studying language fluidity and by grounding these discussions in situated ethnographies that showcase the affordances of combining and blending languages and modalities simultaneously, I hope to expand work in multimodality to further consider the value of linguistic diversity. In addition, by illustrating how multilinguals leverage digital and analog modes, I suggest that conversations about language diversity and linguistic fluidity could benefit from further acknowledging multimodalities as critical components of students' linguistic repertoires. Through this work, I present methods and theoretical models of language and writing that reflect the diverse communicative practices of contemporary classrooms and workplaces, thus extending and contributing to Adam Banks's call to "build theories, pedagogies, and practices of multimedia writing that honor the traditions and thus the people who are still too often not present in our classrooms, on our faculties, [and] in our scholarship" (14). By bridging multilingualism and multimodality in research and pedagogy, we can "commit fully to altering our pedagogical and research practices—to consider how concretely engaging with different modes, genres, materials, cultural practices, communicative technologies, and language varieties impacts our abilities to make and negotiate meaning, how it impacts both what and how we come to know, and perhaps most importantly, how it might provide us with still other options for knowing and being, and for being known" (Shipka, "Transmodality," 251).

In this chapter, I describe how I blended multilingual/multimodal methods and methodologies to study translation moments at two different research sites. After providing a short overview of emerging studies engaging with multilingual/multimodal research, I briefly introduce my two sites of study, describing how the relationships developed with my communities guide and inform my analysis and presentation of translation moments and A Revised Rhetoric of Translation. Finally, I describe the specific methods and emerging analytical frameworks that I used to identify, analyze, and visualize the rhetoric embedded in translation moments across contexts.

Multilingual, Multimodal Methods and Methodologies

Recent studies illustrate different ways that students work across languages and modes simultaneously in their daily interactions, both in and outside of the writing classroom (Alvarez; Jiménez et al.; Jordan; Kramsch; Lorimer Leonard). These scholars draw from a variety of disciplines to trace students' composing practices beyond the limitations of standardized written English. For example, drawing from the extensive work of Ofelia García and other sociolinguists (e.g., Jan Blommaert), Steven Alvarez studies how "bilingual youth [act] as language brokers for homework in immigrant families," layering several semiotic resources and practices to translate communication between their parents and teachers, to help both parties understand each other (326).

To analyze translanguaging, Alvarez draws from Shirley Brice Heath's concept of a "literacy event," an analytical unit in which writing, reading, or speaking mediate participants' agencies and relationships (Heath, 200, qtd. in Alvarez, 329). Stemming from the notion of literacy events, Alvarez proposes "translanguaging events" as an analytical unit for examining how writers adapt ideas across languages and modes. Translanguaging events, Alvarez explains, are "multilingual collaborative practices [of] shuttling between languages while responding to texts situated in local contexts" (329–30). Examining translanguaging events through an ethnographic study (including interviews, observations, and textual analyses of student work), Alvarez illustrates how translanguaging pedagogies can be implemented into classrooms "by inviting students to language broker, translate, paraphrase, and code-switch, reflexively calling attention to language differences for discussion and analysis" (337).

Similarly calling attention to the translation practices of multilinguals in classroom spaces, Rebecca Lorimer Leonard illustrates how learners who regularly move between languages exhibit an acute "rhetorical attunement" that helps them communicate effectively across modes and with diverse audiences. Drawing on Canagarajah's discussion of translanguaging as a process of "recontextualization," Lorimer Leonard argues that communicative resources are "externally influenced and socially practiced" (232). Based on her analysis of life history interviews, Lorimer Leonard suggests that multilingual writers' linguistic transitions help them develop unique rhetorical strategies to navigate communication (228). These linguistic experiences and developed rhetorical strategies expand multilinguals' "attunement," or orientation, to communication, allowing these writers to leverage a wide range of semiotic resources to reach their audiences effectively. As Lorimer Leonard concludes, in communicative situations, "monolingual writers hear a note; multilingual writers hear a chord" (243). While Lorimer Leonard does not specifically reference multimodality, the layering of semiotic resources used by multilingual communicators in her study echoes the "rhetorical sensitivity" emphasized by scholars in multimodal composition (Ball, Arola, and Sheppard; Shipka).

In his situated analysis of multilingual and multimodal literacy practices in Israeli society, Steven Fraiberg proposes "code mashing" as a framework for describing "the complex blending of multimodal and multilingual texts and literacy practices in our teaching and research" (102). Drawing on theories of literacy ecologies, knotworking, remediation, and actant-network theory, Fraiberg offers rhetoric and composition a way to conceptualize "language as situated, dynamic, heterogeneous, co-constitutive, and contested" (104). Through this analysis, Fraiberg illustrates how writers negotiate "complex arrays of languages, texts, tools, objects, symbols, and tropes" as they move more fluidly than ever across metaphorical and physical boundaries between languages, modalities, nations, and other composing contexts (107).

In table 1, I present just a few examples of some recent methods used to study multilingual/multimodal composing. While no means exhaustive, the table illustrates the similarities in the methods that have been used to study the blending of languages and modes in writing, as well as the relatively small sample sizes represented across these studies. As evidenced in table 1, some studies exploring multilingualism and multimodality together have relied heavily on interviews, observations, and analyses of texts or other artifacts. While these methods are incredibly valuable and have contributed greatly to our understanding of linguistic diversity, some of these methods also seem to privilege the "product" of translation rather than valuing the process. Further, as table 1 shows, some studies threading

Table 1. Methods Used to Study Multilingualism and Multimodality in Rhetoric and Composition

Author	Participants	Methods
Alvarez	10 families (10 mothers, 22 children)	Observations / field notes Interviews Textual/artifact analysis
Barton and Lee	various	Observations / field notes Interviews Autoethnography/storytelling Textual/artifact analysis
Berry, Hawisher, and Selfe	12	Interviews Autoethnography/storytelling Textual/artifact analysis
Canagarajah, "Negotiating"	one class (number of students not specified)	Observations Field notes Interviews Textual/artifact analysis
Canagarajah, "Rhetoric"	1	Textual/artifact analysis
Fraiberg	unspecified	Observations Field notes Interviews Autoethnography/storytelling Textual/artifact analysis
Kramsch	10	Observations Field notes Interviews Autoethnography/storytelling Textual/artifact analysis Surveys
Lorimer Leonard	6	Interviews Textual/artifact analysis

the connections between multilingualism and multimodality tend to have a relatively small number of study participants (perhaps due to the important in-depth, longitudinal nature of this work), limiting our insight into the practices of a handful of students or professionals at a time.

For example, Canagarajah ("Rhetoric") studies one student's translanguaging practices through the student's written products. Barry, Hawisher, and Selfe's use of video recordings to capture twelve student narratives pushes toward a more situated study of multilingualism and multimodality, by providing an additional layer of understanding in reference to students' multilingual, multimodal composing practices. Together, these scholars have developed important frameworks and methods to understand the intersections of multimodality and multilingualism. Yet I would argue that more work needs to be done to develop situated multimodal coding methods or replicable processes for analysis that account for the blending of languages and modalities simultaneously during multilingual composing processes.

Using emerging work that highlights the connections between multilingualism and multimodality (e.g., the similarities in method depicted in table 1) and drawing on methods from rhetoric and composition and from technical communication in my ongoing collaborations with over fifty-five participants across two research sites, I analyzed how individuals move across languages and modalities simultaneously through translation moments. Through the present study's discussion of that work, I argue that translation moments help us understand how and when individuals leverage rhetorical resources to transform information from one language or discourse to another, thus providing researchers with an additional framework for studying language fluidity in ways that are culturally and rhetorically situated. Developing replicable methods and processes for analyzing multilingualism and multimodality in practice can help us expand our approaches to teaching and researching writing and communication outside the boundaries of named languages, alphabetic modalities, and disciplinary-specific conventions.

Research Sites: Translation Moments in and across Latinx Communities

To understand how multilingual and multimodal practices are enacted during translation moments, I worked with two communities of translators over a period of three years. I expand on the research sites and their respective communities in chapters 5 and 6. Rather than working with participants who speak languages in which I am not fluent, I specifically chose to work with Latinx translators who work across Spanishes and Englishes. To make arguments about the connections between language, identity, culture, and technology and to honor the role that identity plays in the negotiation of multimodality and multilingualism, I have to acknowledge and leverage my own positionality in this analysis; that I identify as a South American emergent bilingual (García and Li Wei) (more specifically, as a person who can speak Englishes and Spanishes to equal capacities but learned to speak English as a second language) inherently influences the way that I interacted with my participants and analyzed their practices. Although my training in rhetoric and technical communication might be useful to some degree if I were to navigate multilingual contexts with languages that are unfamiliar to me (e.g., French, Arabic, etc.), that I speak Spanish and identify as a Latina affords me an analytical frame of reference that would not be present if I was analyzing the work of participants in another language. For this reason, while I acknowledge the colonial histories embedded in both Spanish and English, I chose to work with communities with which I identify, namely immigrant, Latinx individuals who speak Spanish. In this way, I can use these relationships with my participants to present a more nuanced and thorough analysis that accounts for multilingual/multimodal processes, products, and lived experiences.

To study the rhetorical choices and decisions that communicators made during their process of translation, it was important for me to work with multilingual communicators who work as translators in various contexts, both within and outside of academia. Although we can argue that any communicator from any linguistic and cultural background(s) experiences translation moments, I wanted to work with individuals who have various degrees and training in the long-standing profession of translation. Grounding conversations discussing language fluidity in rhetoric and composition with conversations in translation studies and technical communication can help researchers further understand the multilingual, multimodal language transformation practices that are taking place in our classrooms and professional spaces.

To illustrate the rhetorical activities embedded in translation, chapters 5 and 6 present stories from my work with two organizations: Knightly Latino News, a bilingual, student-run organization in news broadcasting, located at the University of Central Florida; and the Language Services Department, a small translation and interpretation business, located within the Hispanic Center of Western Michigan, a nonprofit organization serving Latinx communities in Grand Rapids. Although I reference the translators in these organizations as participants throughout this book, the people in these two organizations have become part of my family in so many material ways. While the period of data collection for this particular project was approximately three years, the period of relationship building that allowed this project to come to fruition was much longer. Without the relationships, the analysis presented in this book would be inaccurate and superficial at best, not encompassing the trust and mutual commitment to Latinx representations that will continue to support the efforts of this project beyond the publication of this particular monograph. None of this work would have been possible without the ideas and active contributions of the translators whose stories are featured on every page of this book. Every piece of this project is a product of a participatory methodology that centers the stories and *testimonios*[1] of Latinx communities as integral to the gathering and representation of data (Torrez, "Translating").

My goal in working with both of the organizations included in this project was to build relationships that would help us (me and the members of each organization) collectively highlight the multilingual, multimodal communicative strategies enacted by translators in their daily work activities. Because these communities reflect various aspects of my own identity as a multilingual, I approached this project as a reciprocal act that allowed both me and my participants to highlight various aspects of our relationships to meet our own goals. I did not approach either organization only to advance my own research agenda; the purpose of our partnerships was to build community and find multifaceted ways of representing our collective work across languages and modalities, for my own purposes as a researcher, for my participants' purposes as members of organizations that need publicity and funding, and for our collective purposes as human beings working to navigate communication in English-dominant spaces in and outside of the United States. As I present the data of this project in the remaining chapters, I weave my own analysis and interpretation with my participants' stories, perspectives, and *testimonios*.

Method

One of my primary goals in sharing this project is to highlight the importance of using multimodal, multilingual methods to study multimodal, multilingual practices. Following Shipka's call (in *Toward a Composition*) to move from merely seeing and assessing multimodal products toward a further understanding of the multimodal process, I argue for a multimodal methodology that leverages visual methods to clearly illustrate the value of multilingual communication. I want to move from simply analyzing final products of translation to visualizing the processes and practices of translation themselves, including the voices and experiences of translators within my analytical framework. To do so, I blend a variety of visual methods in my data collection practices, using video and audio recordings, as well as visuals and diagrams, and presenting my data both through written dialogue and through brief video montages and visualizations, further introduced in chapters 3–6.

Many scholars in rhetoric and composition and in technical communication have discussed the value of visual methods and methodologies (Brumberger; McKee and DeVoss; Hawisher et al.). As Hawisher et al. explain, visual methods (including, in their case, the use of video recordings) "add additional semiotic information and more to alphabetic representations of research." In addition, visual research methods can support data collection and analysis in ways that account for and highlight the embodied and embodying nature of interactions (Gonzales, "Multimodality," "Using ELAN"). Although I do not consider myself a visual designer or filmmaker, I have followed emerging calls for visual methods and technical communication by incorporating visual methods of data collection and analysis to help me understand data in various dimensions beyond the limitations of written language; that is, I use visual methods not only to account for what my participants were doing during my data collection periods but also to understand and acknowledge the environments, locations, and positionality of this work within their broader rhetorical and cultural contexts (Pigg). In table 2, I provide an overview of the specific methods used to collect visual data in this project. These methods borrow from scholarship in rhetoric and composition as well as in technical communication, thus leveraging the multiple ways that multilingual, multimodal communication has been studied and practiced across disciplines.

As evidenced in table 2, the methods employed in this project yielded 449 hours of data, not including the three years of physical observation and the relationship building encompassed in the various stages of this project. My data collection processes were not only granted clearance from an institutional review board but also adhere to the professional ethical standards of the American Translators Association and received multiple recursive cycles of consent from all participants involved in the project. All personal information included in translation documents was protected

Table 2. Multimodal Methods of Data Collection

Method	Amount Collected	Description
Screencast recordings	30 hours	Screencast recordings allow researchers to record participants' computer screens as they compose, noting where participants click and how they move their cursors on-screen (Slattery; Pigg). This situated method was particularly useful for analyzing how participants coordinated digital resources to complete translation projects in digital contexts.
Video footage	403 hours	Although screencast recordings allow me to see what participants are doing on their computer screens, this method was not sufficient in accounting for participants' embodied practices (Pigg). For this reason, I installed video cameras at my two research sites, not only to record what participants were doing as they translated on their computers but also to see how participants were using their bodies to transform information.
Artifact-based interviews	16 hours	While the screencasts provided an illustration of participant's digital movements (e.g., mouse clicks, typing), the screencasts do not provide insights into participants' motivations for making these moves; that is, the screencast data allowed me to see what sources and tools students were using to translate, but they did not explain why participants chose to use these resources (Blythe and Gonzales). For this reason, each of the participants was asked to participate in a follow-up artifact-based interview, where the participant and I watched the screencasts together and discussed why the participant chose to make specific moves during the digital translation process. For example, I asked participants why they decided to use or not use a particular definition or why they went to a particular website. In this way, artifact-based interviews provided an additional layer of analysis for understanding my participants' translation practices.
Field observations	150 pages collected over three years	In addition to the video footage and screen recordings, I used a field notebook to write down specific moments of translation during my observation at two different research sites. Using this notebook to sketch specific instances and to write time frames during the video recording allowed me to streamline my analysis and to make space for my own interpretive lens during the data collection process.
TOTAL	449 hours	

and stored in encrypted servers. Due to the reciprocal research methodology and analytical methods embraced in this project, participants at both of my research sites asked that their names not be changed in this manuscript, provided that all drafts were shared and approved by participants before final publication. By keeping my participants' names in the manuscript and by referring my partnering organizations by name, I seek to give additional credit to the people who inform this work and to provide those organizations with tangible representations of their involvement in this project. All publications related to this project, including but not limited to this monograph, are cited and distributed by individuals at both of my research cites (at community events, on grant applications, and in other materials). In this way, these publications are shared as examples of our collective work together, rather than merely as representations of my authorship or research agenda.

At both research sites, I triangulated my methods of data collection and data analysis with my participants' own descriptions and practices. As I recorded and analyzed how participants navigated translation moments (to visualize the actual practices of translation), I asked for feedback from my participants during semi-structured artifact-based interviews and during more informal conversations on observation days. During these feedback moments, I asked participants to describe their translation practices in their own words, and I then incorporated this discussion into my evolving coding scheme. The coding scheme I present was developed both through my own analysis and through conversations and data triangulation exercises with fifty-five participants.

I went through three rounds of coding to analyze my data. First, I coded data to identify the frequency and length of translation moments as they took place at both research cites. Second, I went through a round of coding using a preliminary coding scheme developed through a pilot study that I conducted with user-experience researcher Rebecca Zantjer (see Gonzales and Zantjer). In that pilot study, we developed a preliminary list of codes that we could expect to see when coding how multilingual communicators navigated rhetorical decisions during translation moments. For instance, we learned that when analyzing translation moments, we would frequently find multilingual communicators using gestures or drawing sketches to communicate ideas with various audiences. We also learned that multilinguals would sometimes tell stories during translation moments, to illustrate how they have experienced specific words, ideas, or concepts in previous interactions. During this second round of coding, I used the preliminary coding scheme developed with Rebecca, while simultaneously looking for additional patterns that emerged from my data (Saldaña). I adjusted my coding scheme to reflect the specific patterns that I was seeing participants use to navigate translation moments at my two new research sites. I then went through a third round of coding with my revised coding scheme, where I also triangulated my analysis with my participants through the artifact-based interviews.

Ultimately, after three rounds of coding, I identified 2,871 translation moments that took place across both research sites during my data collection period. In analyzing these translation moments in collaboration with my participants, we identified 5,734 second-tier codes describing what took place as translators made decisions during translation moments; that is, while there were close to three thousand translation moments in my data, each translation moment often encompassed the use of more than one rhetorical strategy on the part of the translator. For example, participants used digital translation tools, such as Google Translate or Linguee (an online dictionary), to find options for their translations. Often, these digital translation tools alone did not provide adequate translations for my participants' projects. In addition, translators deployed other semiotic resources and rhetorical strategies to translate information—reading aloud, sketching, gesturing, and/or storytelling across languages to accomplish their work. These rhetorical strategies, or second-tier codes, are further described in table 3 and represent the activities and practices that translators used to navigate translation moments as they decided how to translate a specific word or phrase in a specific rhetorical situation.

The eight codes or strategies presented in table 3 represent the discreet activities most frequently used by translators to navigate translation moments. As evidenced in the table, these strategies contain multimodal components to various degrees. For instance, gesturing, or the use of your body to signal meaning, encompasses multimodality in that it requires participants to move beyond words in their description of ideas (Arola and Wysocki; Shipka, *Toward a Composition*). Although gesturing strategies do not necessarily entail the use of digital technologies, these strategies represent emerging definitions of "digital" writing, echoing Angela Haas's argument (in "Wampum as Hypertext") that digital technologies begin with our fingers and our bodies' movement. To understand the affordances of digital writing, Haas contends what we must account for both the material tools through which digital writing happens and the cultural/rhetorical contexts in which this work takes place. Hence, as I analyzed translation moments, I aimed to understand both what was taking place on my participants' screens while they typed information and what was taking place in the physical environment that housed the translation offices. In this way, I could account for what Ann-Shivers McNair describes as "bodies and knowledge in the making," specifically by paying attention to how participants were interacting with various technologies, with each other, and with their own experiences as they composed across languages. As Gabriela Raquel Ríos clarifies in her discussion of Nahua rhetorics ("Performing"), "we must struggle to (re)consider the separation between metaphor and materiality with respect to space in a literal fashion" (87), understanding that "knowledge is formed vis-à-vis *relationships*" with ourselves, each other, and the land (86).

Similarly, translation strategies such as "repeating" and "storytelling"

Table 3. Final Coding Scheme (Second-Tier Codes)

Code	Description
Use of Digital Translation Tools	Digital translation tools used by participants in this project include Google Translate, Linguee, a Spanish–English dictionary, and WordReference, a bilingual synonym finder.
Deconstructing	Deconstruction strategies include word conjugation or adaptation, when participants take an initial word and adapt it to meet the context of a single sentence or section in the translation.
Gesturing	Gesturing strategies include the "gesticulations on the fly" (McNeill) made by participants as they discuss a word or phrase during a translation moment.
Reading Aloud	Reading aloud is used by participants when they are testing if their translation "makes sense" in the context of an entire document. Participants frequently read their translations aloud several times to ensure accuracy.
Negotiating	Negotiating strategies were often used in conjunction with the use of digital translation tools. Participants negotiated when they were deciding between possible options for translating a single word.
Storytelling	Storytelling took place when participants would have a conversation about how to translate a specific word or phrase. In these instances, participants would tell stories about how they have heard or used a word or phrase in the past.
Repeating	Often, participants would repeat a word or phrase several times during a translation moment. Through this repetition, participants cued their own indexed cultural knowledge, deciding which word "sounded right" based on the ways in which they have heard that word used in previous contexts.
Sketching	Sketching strategies were used when participants tried to make sense of a word by drawing a figure or object. These strategies were often used when participants tried to explain a concept to another translator in order to come to a common understanding.

do not always require traditional conceptions of digital tools and technologies. However, these strategies were frequently accompanied by gestures and coupled with research that took place in online environments, as participants Googled, downloaded, and manipulated images, videos, and other information to help them understand particular concepts and ideas in both Spanish and English. As they decide how to best say or write a word in a different language, translators have to recall their previous experiences hearing and saying specific words and phrases, reliving their histories in order to make information accessible in a new language. Thus, to understand translation as a multimodal activity, it is important to account for all the elements embedded in translation moments—elements that encompass the intricate layering of semiotic resources in recursive, iterative cycles. As I further demonstrate in the remaining chapters of this book, translation is a multimodal activity not only because it increasingly requires the navigation of digital technologies but also because it requires the rhetorical coordination of semiotic resources beyond alphabetic language. Understanding multimodal communication through translation can help researchers, teachers, and practitioners further understand how languages, modalities, and media intersect in the rhetorical work enacted by multilinguals.

3 • Translation as a Multimodal Practice

> Your desire for order and meaning prompts you to track the ongoing
> circumstances of your life, to sift, sort, and symbolize your experiences and
> try to arrange them into a pattern and story that speak to your reality. You
> scan your inner landscape, books, movies, philosophies, mythologies, and the
> modern sciences for bits of lore you can patch together to create a new
> narrative articulating your personal reality. You scrutinize and question
> dominant and ethnic ideologies and the mind-sets their cultures induce in
> others. And, putting all the pieces together, you re-envision the map of the
> known world, creating a new description of reality and scripting a new story.
> (Anzaldúa, 545)

As I briefly explain in chapter 2, my analysis of translation moments helped
me further understand and forge connections between multilingualism
and multimodality. By intricately coding and visualizing how translators
adapt information across languages, I was able to both see and experience
the rhetorical coordination of modes that takes place as multilingual communicators transform ideas from one language to another. Because language is constantly in motion, the words that we use to describe specific
concepts or ideas shift and transform with our cultural norms and practices. To maintain expertise in language transformation, translators have to
echo this flexibility and fluidity, constantly changing their practices as languages and linguistic patterns evolve. As I further illustrate in this chapter,
translators and other multilingual communicators practice and hone rhetorical skills and strategies in multilingual/multimodal communication
(Frost and Blum Malley; Fraiberg; Gonzales, "Multimodality").

Translation is a multimodal practice in that it requires

1. decentering of alphabetic language and of alphabetic, written
   language in English (what some scholars describe as "standardized

written English") as the single or most important element of communicative practice (Horner, Selfe, and Lockridge);

2. rhetorical awareness of how modalities and genres function in different contexts and for various audiences (Arola, Ball, and Sheppard, "Multimodality");

3. purposeful and rhetorical layering of modes and media, with critical attention to how modes like visuals, sounds, and words work together in creating meaning for various stakeholders (Takayoshi and Selfe); and

4. critical understanding of how communicative practice is always rhetorically and culturally situated (Kress, *Multimodality*; Guerra; Shipka, *Toward a Composition*).

In this chapter, I draw on these connections and further discuss the multimodal elements embedded in contemporary translation processes. I first provide emerging definitions of multimodality and then discuss how these definitions of multimodality have recently acknowledged connections to multilingual communication, all in an effort to continue pushing conceptions of writing in rhetoric and composition beyond standardized written English (SWE). Finally, I will argue that a closer examination of translation and its multimodal elements can help writing researchers, teachers, and practitioners continue expanding beyond SWE through culturally situated, multimodal/multilingual research.

Defining "Multimodality"

Over the last two decades, there have been numerous ongoing conversations, both in rhetoric and composition and in related fields, regarding what "counts" or what "is considered" multimodality and multimodal communication (Ball, Arola, and Sheppard; Kress; New London Group; Shipka, "Including . . . the Digital," *Toward a Composition*). Multimodality has direct ties to digital technologies and digital media, encompassing the use and manipulation of "still and moving images, animations, color, words, music and sound" in digital contexts (Takayoshi and Selfe, 1). Early conceptions of multimodality, specifically within rhetoric and composition and computers and composition, tied multimodality specifically to writing in digital spaces. For example, the New London Group's 1996 position statement directly stated that "literacy pedagogy must now account for the burgeoning variety of text forms associated with information and multimedia technologies." In its early development, multimodality emerged partly as a consequence of the need to reconceptualize writing beyond alphabetic texts due to the affordances provided by emerging technologies.

As definitions of multimodality continue to shift and emerge, scholars like Jody Shipka, Cynthia Selfe, Cheryl Ball, Kristin Arola, Jennifer Sheppard, and Janine Butler (among many others) remind us that multimodality is always embedded in our communicative practices, includes but is not limited to writing, and is not always bound to using digital tools (Shipka, "Including . . . the Digital"). As Gabriela Raquel Ríos clarifies, multimodality has been practiced in non-Western communities for decades: "Indigenous peoples have historically used music, dance, theater, and other types of nontextual practices to make meaning, and we still do" ("Performing," 89). As Shipka further explains, although the digital elements and possibilities of multimodality are important, "when our scholarship fails to consider, and when our practices do not ask students to consider, the complex and highly distributed processes associated with the production of texts (and lives and people), we run the risk of overlooking the fundamentally multimodal aspects of all communicative practice" (*Toward a Composition*, 13).

Although definitions and arguments for multimodality continue to evolve, the ongoing thread of these conversations links back to the relationship between rhetoric and communication. For instance, in describing their early experiences with multimodality and specifically with teaching and learning multimodal composition, Arola, Ball, and Sheppard explain,

> While we may not have realized it at the time, [in being trained to teach multimodality,] we were being trained not so much as writing teachers, but as teachers of rhetoric. That is, we were mentored away from a singular focus on written text and toward one that integrated modes based on audience, purpose, and context. Such an approach allowed students to better understand the rhetorical situation for which they were communicating and to choose the affordances and means of persuasion best suited to their purposes. ("Multimodality")

Furthermore, as Ball, Arola, and Sheppard elaborate in *Writer/Designer*, whether the use and layering of semiotic practices and resources happens on a screen or in a material space, the key to multimodal communication resides in communicators' rhetorical awareness and ability to navigate different rhetorical situations. This is why teachers and researchers of writing acknowledge the multiple modalities through which students and professionals create and share ideas, particularly (though not exclusively) in digital environments.

Drawing from these definitions of multimodality, I position translation as a multimodal practice not only because it encompasses the use of various modalities and technologies (e.g., visuals, sounds, and words) but, perhaps more important, because it entails the rhetorical navigation of these communicative tools to make meaning and accomplish action across languages and cultures. The connections between modalities, media, and rhetoric that are enacted by translators during translation moments echo contemporary definitions of multimodality, while also highlighting the value of linguistic diversity, foregrounded by researchers studying multilingual communication. In the sections that follow, I elaborate on how translation renders both multimodal and multilingual communication, two areas of study that have been simultaneously helping rhetoric and composition scholarship to research and produce writing outside of English-dominant, alphabetic boundaries.

Multilingualism and Multimodality: A Push beyond SWE

In many ways, through their focus on the fluidity of communication practices and the expansion beyond the limitations of SWE, proponents of multimodality in rhetoric and composition echo the calls of multilingual composition scholars who reject the "myth of linguistic homogeneity" that is sometimes embraced in higher education (Matsuda). As I have argued in other places (Gonzales, "Multimodality"), multilingual and multimodal researchers have worked toward similar (though separated) objectives for many years, pushing for the expansion of rhetoric and composition beyond SWE to further consider the potential of working with diverse composing tools and practices. Yet, until recently, conversations connecting multilingualism and multimodality in rhetoric and composition have remained largely separate, with a few notable exceptions (e.g., Fraiberg; Frost and Blum Malley; Horner, Selfe, and Lockridge; Shipka, "Transmodality").

For example, in "Translinguality, Transmodality, and Difference," Horner, Selfe, and Lockridge provide a visualization of how the terms *multilingual* and *multimodal* have been used in parallel isolation: "A search of *CCC* titles and abstracts identifies 50 instances of the term 'multimodal,' dating from 1991 to the present, and 34 instances of the term 'multilingual' dating from 1990 forward." These terms have been used separately in rhetoric and composition to continue pushing against what Horner, Selfe, and

Lockridge define as the "single language / single modality" approach to writing, which limits communication in writing classrooms to SWE. Horner, Selfe, and Lockridge replace the prefix in the terms *multilingualism* and *multimodality* with the prefix *trans-* (i.e., *translingualism, transmodality*), in an effort to move away from the additive model of language that positions each "language" or "mode" as a stable, fixed entity. In the same piece, Horner argues for a "focus on work across boundaries of language and modality rather than seeing our task as one of selecting from a menu of languages and modalities." Ultimately, through their dialogue, Horner, Selfe, and Lockridge conclude that "while all language practice is multimodal (using the terms language, practice, and multimodal as 'mass' nouns), language *practices* are not multimodal in the same ways, and the differences among/between them are significant. A radio play is not the same as a live theater performance or a television broadcast, even though they're all (in quite different ways) multimodal, and the differences are quite significant from the production, distribution, and reception ends."

Drawing on Horner, Selfe, and Lockridge, Shipka ("Transmodality") "insist[s] upon the importance of approaches to composing" that forefront "the translingual and multimodal (or transmodal) character of texts and communicative practices," paying attention to the many ways in which all transmodal communication acts are not created equal and require the deployment of different technical and linguistic abilities and strategies (251). Stemming from these examples, I argue that although all linguistic acts can be considered "multilingual" since they require a blending and movement of discourses as individuals make meaning from person to person, there are stark and wide ranges of difference in multilingual acts. There are differences, for instance, in the multilingual nature of a conversation between two individuals speaking Englishes and a conversation in which individuals are using Englishes and Spanishes.

The key to understanding the connections between multilingualism and multimodality remains in analyzing the rhetorical moves being enacted by individuals who move through fluid linguistic, material, and technological practices in their interactions. If writing teachers and practitioners want to continue pushing beyond the "single language / single modality" approach to writing and communication, we need to continue developing frameworks for understanding how communicative practice functions outside this dichotomy, not only claiming that all communicative acts are polyvocal (i.e., multilingual and multimodal or transmodal), but also intricately understanding how this polyvocality is enacted and practiced (Gilyard). For this reason, analyzing translation, paying attention to how multilingual communicators rhetorically navigate simultaneously across modes and languages to make information accessible for speakers and readers of different languages, can help scholars more thoroughly understand the dimensions of multilingualism and multimodality, as well as the connections between these two areas.

The connections between language and multimodality that are drawn by Horner, Selfe, and Lockridge and by Shipka have been emerging, albeit implicitly, in rhetoric and composition scholarship. Indeed, scholars in multimodality have been referencing all language practices as multimodal (Kress), noting the ways in which writers' interactions with a page inherently require multimodal acts that result in perceivably monomodal alphabetic products. As Shipka elaborates, "The multimodal nature of texts and of literate practices is not new. Rather, what is new is our attention to them" (*Toward a Composition,* 11). Similarly, scholars embracing the "translingual" turn in composition posit that communication is and has always been what some might consider "multilingual." Thus, even the term *multilingual* is unnecessary according to some translingual scholars and may contribute to the essentialization of the linguistic diversity that has been present in our classrooms and workplaces for decades (Horner, Selfe, and Lockridge).

Regardless of how we identify and name language and composing practices, Vivette Milson-Whyte explains, the goal of contemporary researchers should be not only to claim that linguistic and communicative diversity is a reality in contemporary classrooms and workplaces but also to better understand how, when, and why these specific communicative practices are enacted. As Milson-Whyte elaborates, linguistic transitions (e.g., translanguaging) "are sometimes motivated by social dictates, by ignorance, by desires to make one language contest or complement another, or to achieve other specific purposes, or for no apparent reason" (116). The challenge for teachers and researchers interested in multilingualism and multimodality becomes not only acknowledging the presence of linguistic diversity and of communicative diversity through multimodality but also intricately understanding the reasoning and motivation behind these practices. This is where translation serves as a useful model for understanding multilingualism and multimodality in action, as translators make decisions and deliver translations to be used for particular purposes and rhetorical contexts.

Multimodal Elements in Translation: Media, Language, and Culture

Considering the emerging connections between multilingualism and multimodality, I present translation as a multimodal activity in this project for several reasons. First, when translating information, individuals are consistently making rhetorical decisions as they present information to audiences from various linguistic and cultural backgrounds. In making these decisions, translators have to consider the specific histories and backgrounds of their intended audiences, understanding regional and historical variations of specific languages (e.g., Spanishes and Englishes) that might influence how information is perceived in a particular instance or utterance. For example, translators have to use different Spanishes to reach Mexican American audiences from particular socioeconomic backgrounds than they use when translating for Spanish-speaking communities from Spain whose version of Spanish derives from Catalan, a European language used in parts of Spain and France (Torrez, "Somos Mexicanos"). Throughout the translation process, but specifically during translation moments (when rhetorical decisions are most directly navigated), translators have to consider what orientations to language and culture are embraced by their intended audiences, making rhetorical decisions about which words in the translators' linguistic repertoires would be most appropriate to use in specific translation scenarios. Thus, translators move through the various linguistic modalities encompassed in their communicative repertoires, making deliberate rhetorical decisions about which practices to represent in their final translations and which alphabets to draw from to represent ideas to a specific community.

In addition to issues of linguistic variations, contemporary translators have to consider issues of visual design and media when completing translations. When translating a birth certificate or medical record, for instance, translators have to translate both alphabetic information and visual data to render a translation that will be understood by an individual who does not speak the source language used in the original document. Figure 4 presents an example of a government seal that was translated as part of a birth certificate translation project completed at one of my research sites, showing how translations encompass multimodal (visual and alphabetic) elements.

The image at the top of figure 4 is a screenshot of the original document presented in Spanish to the translations office that I worked with during my data collection process. On the bottom is the translated version of this same seal from the Dominican Republic. As figure 4 illustrates, translators working on technical documents such as birth certificates and medical records not only have to translate words from one language to another but also have to redesign visual elements to complete the translation. To ensure that government agencies will accept translated medical documents, translators have to provide mirror translations, which consist of translated doc-

Fig. 4. Original (*top*) and translation (*bottom*) of a birth certificate seal from the Dominican Republic

uments that identically match the design, layout, and formatting of the original text (Pym, qtd. in Gonzales and Turner, 16). To create mirror translations, translators practice multimodality, by making decisions about how to redesign texts in a way that will be understood both alphabetically and visually by readers from various linguistic and cultural backgrounds.

In addition to incorporating visual design elements, much of the translation work currently enacted in professional offices (e.g., the offices depicted in this project) takes place in digital spaces, through the combination of various digital tools. Indeed, all the written translations that I analyzed for this project required the use of digital resources and platforms (e.g., digital translation tools, word-processing software, and design applications). As Lyons (19–20) elaborates, contemporary translators now adopt digital tools for many purposes, including the following:

- Creating templates and processing data uniformly to leverage for future use
- Improving the efficacy of data processing to save time and money

- Standardizing data capture so that modifications can be implemented in real time
- Providing data that can be retrieved instantly to safeguard patient safety further and improve public health monitoring of drug safety (pharmacovigilance)
- Minimizing human error and omissions to ensure data accuracy and prevent data loss

Thus, the use and adaptation of digital tools is a frequent site of interaction for translation activities, resulting in further multimodal navigation across languages and digital platforms. Although digital tools are vital for short technical translations, such as birth certificates, the diversity of these tools only increases in more complex and extensive translation projects, leading to increased need for technological expertise in contemporary translators (Gonzales and Turner).

While the rhetorical decision-making needed to adapt information across languages is multimodal in that it requires the purposeful combination and adaptation of semiotic resources in both physical and digital contexts, the identities and lived experiences of the specific translators introduced in this project also play a role in their multimodal, multilingual work. Issues of identity and culture are critical to understanding the motivations behind translation and the connections between multilingualism and multimodality. Just as multimodal communication cannot be abstracted from its rhetorical contexts (Ball, Arola, and Sheppard), translation, as a multilingual/multimodal process, cannot be separated from the rhetorical contexts in which it happens. To understand translation and to further acknowledge the connections that translators build between multilingualism and multimodality, it is important to account for the roles of culture(s) and language(s) in these interactions.

Translation as Culturally Situated Multilingualism and Multimodality

In addition to working across various digital tools and platforms, translators navigating translation moments make rhetorical decisions about how to best represent their past experiences in new contexts. For example, during a translation moment, a translator pauses to decide between two or three different variations of a word that could be used to translate a specific term from a source language (e.g., English) to a target language (e.g., Spanish). To see an example of this, try using Google Translate or any other digital translation tool to translate a specific word into another language.

In most cases, the digital translation software will provide you with several options for your translation, much like a thesaurus. During translation moments, individuals frequently combine the options that may be rendered through a digital translation tool with translation options and communicative practices that they can recall from their previous experiences.

During translation moments, translators may ask themselves, "Should I use *this* word or *that* word to represent the English word or concept in Spanish? What would make *most* sense to this specific community? What adaptations should I make to this word in order for it to fit in this sentence?" For instance, in the example of a translation moment introduced in chapter 1, Sandra asked herself if she should use the word *mazorca* or the word *choclo* when mentioning corn on the cob to her audience, since either word can mean "corn" in Spanish. In her present rhetorical situation, Sandra decided to pause within her discussion and explain how the word *mazorca* had been previously misinterpreted in another context, using her previous experience with a word to make an informed decision during a new translation moment. During this translation moment, Sandra combined her memory of a previous linguistic experience with a visual aid (i.e., a picture of corn on the cob), to guarantee that her audience would understand the type of corn that she referenced in her presentation.

Like Sandra's example, as translators make decisions during translation moments, they are pushed to think about how they have used, heard, and adapted words in previous contexts. In addition to thinking about how to use a word at a specific moment for a particular audience, translators also consider where and when they have heard words before and how they have previously navigated a similar translation. These questions, though often harmless, can sometimes trigger powerful memories that bring people back to their previous linguistic and cultural experiences, causing them to relive communicative negotiations in order to make an informed translation decision in their current rhetorical situation (Guerra). Over time, the process of leveraging memories into productive action during new translation projects helps multilingual communicators develop a unique, culturally situated orientation to multimodal, multilingual communication, an orientation that can be accounted for through what I call "A Revised Rhetoric of Translation." In particular, because translators are always drawing on all their linguistic and communicative tools, resources, and memories to make meaning in new contexts, they maintain a constant state of multilingual/multimodal awareness, caused by both the privilege and the imposition of always having to live "in between" cultural and linguistic markers.

In *This Bridge We Call Home* (Anzaldúa and Keating), Gloria Anzaldúa describes the process through which multilingual communities of color, particularly Mexican-American Chicanxs, navigate communication in and across linguistic, cultural, and physical borderlands. Being both American and Mexican, some Chicanxs operate through a constant state of "in-betweenness," what Anzaldúa refers to as a "mestiza consciousness,"[1] the understanding that because you come from the Mexico/U.S. borderland, you never really "fit" into a single language, place, or culture. Chicanx communities are always in a state of pushing and rejecting binaries and boundaries, fighting to fit in, whether they are trying to fit into Mexican identities that reject both Indigenous roots and ties to U.S. Englishes or into white American culture that frequently rejects and oppresses Mexican identities and Indigenous languages and people. Thus, to communicate and accomplish work in between identities, Chicanx people and other historically marginalized communities inherently work outside the boundaries of the "single language / single modality" spectrum, particularly because their own languages and practices have been historically excluded from mainstream communicative spaces in the United States. In turn, Anzaldúa explains, Chicanxs experience a non-Western, nonlinear or normed journey to knowledge and understanding, what she calls *conocimiento*—a journey that prompts them to develop communicative practices that inherently reject and do not fit into a single identity or linguistic category.

Anzaldúa describes *conocimiento* through seven stages that guide how Chicanxs develop and sustain methods of knowing and self-understanding. These stages of coming into being, as Anzaldúa explains, are inherently multilingual and multimodal, as "conocimiento questions conventional knowledge's current categories, classifications, and content," thus expanding beyond and across single, English-dominant, alphabetic categories of communication (Anzaldúa, 541). Linguistic practices experienced by Chicanxs, such as translation, are experienced "neither" entirely in one language or practice "nor" entirely in another, representing an "in-between" space of communication that blends languages and practices for specific "audience[s], purpose[s], and context[s]" (Arola, Ball, and Sheppard, "Multimodality"). *Conocimiento*, or coming into knowledge and understanding as a Chicanx, requires a transgression of any single language or identity marker, requiring communicators to draw both on their Indigenous roots and knowledge-making practices and on the experiences and frameworks of the Western colonizers.

In the same way that concepts like "multimodality" and "translingualism" reject the idea of a standard or normed set of communicative practices, *conocimiento* works outside of communicative boundaries and binaries, having no singular path to knowledge making and transmission. *Conocimiento* (and, I argue, translation) is "a form of spiritual inquiry," reached through a layering and movement across "creative acts—writing, art-making, dancing, healing, teaching, meditation, and spiritual activism—both mental and somatic (the body, too, is a form as well as a site of creativity)" (Anzaldúa, 541–42). Hence, the way that Anzaldúa describes the meaning-making practices of *conocimiento* can be directly tied to (and extend) definitions of multimodality proposed by rhetoric and composition scholars, situating multimodal practice in multilingual and translingual contexts that reject the limitations of standardized named languages (e.g., SWE). Because Chicanxs are always translating words, cultural norms, and practices (both for themselves and for their communities), they are constantly operating from a multilingual/multimodal orientation.

Indeed, while the connections between languages and modalities are recently emerging in academic scholarship, "embodied ways of knowing" outside academic spaces have always encompassed, particularly for Indigenous communities, the co-constitution of multimodal elements in languaging, remembering, and learning, through dance, theater, and labor with the land (Ríos, "Cultivating," 65). Therefore, further interrogating multimodality through the lenses of race, culture, and identity can help "disrupt the rhetorical velocity of neocolonial rhetorics and practices," allowing academic disciplines to expand their understanding of writing and technology beyond Western, English-dominant and alphabetically dominated frameworks (Haas, "American Indian Rhetorics Pedagogy," 191).

In "Wampum as Hypertext," Angela Haas presents a counterhistory to Western notions of technology and hypertext, explaining that normed, Western conceptions of hypertext center on positivist orientations to technology that value digital contexts over material realities. Explaining that "both Western and wampum hypertexts employ digital rhetoric to communicate nonlinear information," Haas describes the etymology of the word *digital* as stemming from our digits, our fingers, the original creators of multimodal, hypertextual composition. Through her discussion of wampum's hyptertextual qualities, Haas presents an American Indian tradition of multimedia practice, illustrating how wampum belts trace and reference nonlinear arguments by using various modalities and practices. Thus, Haas illustrates how American Indian traditions enact multimodal communication, particularly in the layering and repositioning of communicative practices to make meaning in specific, culturally relevant rhetorical situations.

Orienting to digital rhetoric through the perspective of African American Rhetorics, Adam Banks also draws connections between culture, history, embodied practice, and multimodality, illustrating how African American practices are carried through contexts and media by DJs (disc jockeys) who remix, repurpose, and reshare stories in and for their communities. Multimodal elements like remixing, sampling, and storytelling have been central to the study and practice of African American Rhetorics for decades, as evidenced through the work of such scholars as Geneva Smitherman, Elaine Richardson, and Gwendolyn Pough, who push our disciplines to recognize the rhetorical labor embedded in African American Languages and practices. Through his work, Banks urges scholars and teachers to continue "building assignments that invite students not only to work across modalities but also to link those multiple modalities, individual assignments, and assignment cycles in critical examination of the power relations and material conditions inscribed in technological tools, networks, and discourses" (165).

Understanding multimodal composition through intersectional cultural-rhetorical frameworks like those presented by Haas, Ríos, and Banks requires that we account for the lived experiences of the people enacting these practices, noting the various cultures, languages, and spaces through which these multimodal practices were developed. We cannot just think of modalities and multimodalities as those that are visually represented or representable through Western ideologies. To understand the full potential of multimodality and its ability to expand notions of writing beyond the Western alphabet, we have to consider the modalities that we cannot always see—those that rest on the bodies and memories of people enacting multimodal acts of survival in various contexts (Leon; Ríos). In this way, we can continue to situate our understanding of rhetoric, knowledge making, and communication "in a knowing and know how that is developed out of our material lives" (Leon, 169).

•	In positioning translation as a multimodal practice, I seek to connect multilingual, multimodal composing practices to specific cultural and linguistic histories. We can understand how multilingualism and multimodality are connected as theoretical frameworks, but to expand conversations connecting multilingualism and multimodality (as well as translingualism and transmodality), it is important to examine how modes and languages are deployed and enacted in practice, through real-life exigencies situated within the lived experiences and daily activities of contemporary communicators. To further understand the connections between multilingualism and multimodality, it is important to move beyond theoretical frameworks and conceptions, to multimodal representations of how these theories are enacted in practice, through translation activities.

In *Toward a Composition Made Whole*, Shipka calls for closer research in the dimensions of multimodality, cautioning against a privileging of multimodal products without an acknowledgment of multimodal processes. As Shipka notes, rhetoric and composition researchers and teachers cannot "fail to trace the complex ways that texts come to be" (13). Thus, much like I expressed concern regarding the limitations of only analyzing multilingual products in composition, Shipka warns against a bias that may be enacted if we only consider multimodal products in student work instead of valuing the multimodal practices that make all writing coming to life in our classrooms. To this warning, I would add that it is important to both consider the multimodal processes leading to multimodal composition and the diverse cultures and identities being negotiated through these practices. As Lisya Seloni posits through her work with multilingual students who engage in multimodal composing, it is important to understand how the linguistic and cultural histories of communicators influence how they develop "alternative rhetorical strategies" that allow them "to engage in a wide range of literacy activities" across languages and modes ("I'm an Artist," 86).

The way in which we blend and use tools, technologies, and platforms is directly dependent on the contexts in which we live and work, relying on the access we have to specific tools and on the histories through which our communicative practices have been shaped and repurposed. In turn, the purpose of multimodal composition is to "provide students [and professionals] with a much broader toolkit from which to function as rhetors in the world," helping them reconceive composing genres and modes, not as static forms that only exist in educational [or professional] settings, but as socially situated heuristics developed to meet the needs of particular communities at specific times (Arola, Ball, and Sheppard, qtd. in Gonzales, "Multimodality").

When we ask students to compose multimodally or when we compose a multimodal text ourselves in a professional capacity, we are not necessarily asking anyone to master a new tool or platform for composing. Instead, situated in sociocultural approaches to writing and design, multimodal composition acknowledges the fluidity of mobile codes embedded in all communicative practice, asking us to think rhetorically about the practices they incorporate in specific contexts when working with specific people.

For this reason, based on the efforts that multilingualism and multimodality make toward expanding communication beyond normed, English-dominant boundaries, translation is inherently a multimodal practice, one that can continue to bridge emerging connections between multimodal and multilingual scholarship and pedagogies. The focus of these connections remains on the rhetorical exigency for continuing to expand conceptions of writing and rhetoric beyond alphabetic, monolingual ideologies in both research and teaching, drawing on linguistic, alphabetic, visual, aural, cultural, and embodied practices as deemed appropriate and necessary in situated rhetorical situations. The goal here is not necessarily to master new technologies or new languages but to strategically make use of whatever communicative practices are available to us in the moment of communication so that we can facilitate understanding both for ourselves and for our various audiences and stakeholders.

Connecting multimodal and multilingual orientations to writing and communication requires us to consider not only the things that we see on paper or on a screen. Multilingual and multimodal composing and the connections between these two frameworks as they are enacted by people of color require an acute awareness of the contextual elements and the rhetorical situations in which these practices happen. To understand how multimodal and multilingual practices intersect in the experiences of people, we have to know more about these experiences than what may be initially present through a written artifact. To understand the multilingual, multimodal "knowledge work" (Grabill) of communities, we have to zoom in on both their practices and the exigencies behind this work (Leon), valuing all elements of composing as equally influential and important.

Having explicated the concept of "translation moments" as an analytical tool for studying the multimodal practices embedded in translation, I turn, in the following chapter, to further introducing the framework of A Revised Rhetoric of Translation, explaining how the translation practices of multilingual communicators can help writing researchers, teachers, and professionals in their efforts to better understand the situated rhetorical work embedded in contemporary multilingual/multimodal communication. While translation moments allow us to see the specific semiotic practices deployed to navigate communicative discrepancy, A Revised Rhetoric of Translation provides us with a broader framework from which to view the entire process of translation in its rhetorical context. Following my discussion of A Revised Rhetoric of Translation in chapter 4, chapters 5 and 6 provide an intricate layering of story and analysis as I present the brilliant work of the communities that allowed me to see multilingual, multimodal communication in action. Through this discussion, I highlight the multimodal elements embedded in translation, including those that entail the use of digital technologies and those that move across embodied and material modes to accomplish work in both academic and professional spaces.

4 • A Revised Rhetoric of Translation

Before presenting my analysis of translation in situated case studies, I want to provide analytical lenses from which to view translation through both microlevel and macrolevel vantage points. As I demonstrate in this chapter, A Revised Rhetoric of Translation serves as a macrolevel orientation to studying language transformation, a framework from which to recognize the ways in which translation work is always situated within a specific cultural-rhetorical situation. By discussing A Revised Rhetoric of Translation, I aim to set up the analytical framework from which we can understand translation moments in the case studies that follow.

To understand how writers, particularly writers from marginalized communities, leverage and layer semiotic practices as they compose across contexts, Michelle Hall Kells explains that we must consider more than what is visible at the time of composition, noting how contextual factors influence both how and what we write, as well as what we use to write in a specific rhetorical situation (87). Kells elaborates,

> Every human interaction—whether in person, print text, cyberspace, or visual media—is a form of intercultural communication. Region of origin, family position, gender, ethnolinguistic identity, nationality, age, and religion are only a few of the variables that constitute one's culture or systems of belonging. Students cannot begin to reconcile differences in cultural systems beyond their own circles of affiliation if they have not critically reflected on their own. (87)

Kells's explicit linking of culture, community, and communication is critical to my own presentation of translation as a culturally situated, multimodal practice, one that requires multilinguals to blend and work across contexts, platforms, and modalities to make meaning both for themselves and for diverse audiences. To illustrate how multilinguals exhibit expertise in multimodal communication, I have to account for all factors involved in translation activities. This includes the writing tools and artifacts involved in translation (e.g., computers, digital translation tools, and word-processing software), as well as the embodied and material conditions that prompt and sustain the translation work. In this way, I can account for multilingual/multimodal interactions at several co-constituted and interwoven levels, including digital and material interfaces as well as physical interactions with tools, technologies, and people. Further, doing this work requires that I rely on the trust and the relationships built with my communities of multilingual participants, those individuals who allowed me to engage with and analyze their practices and experiences through our relationality.

To better understand how multilingualism and multimodality connect through translation, it is important not only to recognize the composing practices of the individual translator but also to acknowledge how these practices are situated in a broader rhetorical context. Conversations about linguistic fluidity often focus entirely on individuals and their linguistic repertoires, without necessarily recognizing the rhetorical situatedness of these languages in (and outside) institutions (Bloom-Pojar; Guerra). As Rachel Bloom-Pojar describes in distinguishing between language orientations in linguistics and in rhetoric, "Saying one 'speaks English' or 'speaks Spanish' acknowledges the importance of an outsider's perspective, reflecting social norms with how others perceive us . . . , and while this may not be the focus of study for linguistics, it is the focus of rhetoric" (19; Bloom-Pojar references Otheguy, García, and Reid, 293). In other words, in rhetoric and composition, we pay attention to the languages that our students speak, not only to understand the individual linguistic histories of students but also to assess and facilitate how these languages are (or are not) leading to effective communication with specific audiences in specific rhetorical contexts. However, it is not enough to ask, welcome, or even require our students to blend languages and modalities in our classrooms; it is important that teachers of writing and rhetoric understand, recognize, and teach how communicative repertoires may be deployed to various degrees for different purposes. This is important whether we are enacting language justice in classrooms settings or building professional practices outside the classroom.

In chapters 5 and 6, I present narratives, visualizations, and examples of how, why, and where multilingual communicators work across language and modes to translate information for their communities, both in academia and in a professional space. To help researchers and teachers recognize how languages and modes are deployed by translators in specific contexts, as well as to help ground the examples that I present in chapters 5 and 6, I further define, in this chapter, what I have come to call "A Revised Rhetoric of Translation." As I describe in the next section, A Revised Rhetoric of Translation, building on our understanding of how multilingual communicators navigate communicative discrepancies during translation moments (chapter 1) and on our acknowledgment of translation as a multimodal activity (chapter 3), furthers our reorientation to language difference and fluidity, specifically by contextualizing the multilingual/multimodal aspects of translation in their surrounding contexts. If we are to understand translation as a multilingual/multimodal practice, it is important for us to acknowledge how linguistic transformations motivate and are influenced by relevant cultural and material elements.

Defining "A Revised Rhetoric of Translation"

A Revised Rhetoric of Translation is a model that I developed (with help from Rebecca Zantjer) through my work with student and professional translators and that I use to present the work of each case study in this project. This model can help us understand language transformation rhetorically, speaking against traditionally held notions of translation as a static, mechanical activity that is disassociated from cultural and historical motivations (what might be described as "a traditional rhetoric of translation"). A Revised Rhetoric of Translation purposely works against the idea that translation can be outsourced or embedded as an afterthought to the intellectual labor of knowledge creation. Rather than thinking of translation as a task that happens only after content is created or developed in one language, this reorientation positions translation as an iterative activity that happens constantly within specific cultures and communities (Agboka; Sun). Further, the revised framework presented in this chapter shows how translation activities are tied to the broader goals and objectives of people and organizations. Through this discussion, A Revised Rhetoric of Translation helps us consider not only the multilingual/multimodal elements that we see taking place during translation moments but also how these visible practices are situated in the histories and experiences of the communities enacting linguistic transformations to meet their goals and objectives.

A Revised Rhetoric of Translation has three pillars that directly speak against traditionally held notions of language as static, isolated, and culturally neutral. These three pillars were developed directly with the participants represented in the case studies within this book in chapters 5 and 6. I here further elaborate on each of the three pillars of this revised rhetoric to illustrate how this reorientation to language diversity can help researchers and teachers not only to theorize policies but to develop methodological frameworks and pedagogical practices that center linguistic diversity in and across cultural-rhetorical contexts.

Pillar 1: Translation is a culturally ~~neutral~~ situated process

Historically, when people talk about translation, they reference the process of taking a word from one language and pairing it with a corresponding word in another language (Batova and Clark). In this model, translation becomes an act of neutral substitution, with the goal being an accurate one-to-one replacement of words in the first language with words in the second language. In the case studies presented in chapters 5 and 6, I break away from this assumption and analyze translation as a culturally situated (rather than neutral) practice, one that expands conceptions of translation from substitution to community-based, rhetorical contextualization.

For example, at my first research site, Knightly Latino News (discussed in chapter 5), student translators illustrate how digital translation software programs such as Google Translate often provide inaccurate and inefficient translations on their own. Digital software only becomes effective through rhetorical manipulations completed by multilingual users who are part of or familiar with the community for whom they are translating. Thus, access to digital dictionaries does not guarantee accurate and culturally situated translations localized for specific communities. To accurately and effectively complete translation work, translators have to navigate digital and material tools within their specific communities, seeking feedback and adjusting their practices to meet the constantly evolving ways through which languages represent the values and ideologies of particular cultures (Gonzales and Zantjer).

In analyzing translation through this revised rhetoric, it is important for us to consider what tools are available in the moment of translation and to understand how these tools both influence and are impacted by translators and the local communities navigating this work. Just like, as scholars in multimodality remind us, we cannot abstract digital tools from their cultural-rhetorical contexts (Banks; Haas), we also cannot abstract language practices from their racial and cultural underpinnings (Gilyard; Guerra). To analyze translation through this revised framework, we need to understand the linguistic transformations taking place during translation moments, as well as the cultural context in which these moments are experienced. To do so, we must consider the tools being used during translation, the specific translation moments experienced in that context, and the lived experiences and history of the particular translators engaging in this work. All of these elements impact the success of the translation project and the experience of the people creating and receiving the translated work.

Pillar 2: Translation is a ~~linear~~ cyclical process

Just as, due to constantly shifting rhetorical practices, translation is not culturally neutral, (effective) translation is also never a "once and done" event. Translation processes are far from linear and involve multiple instances of negotiation and localization (Agboka; Jacquemond; Gonzales and Turner; Ketola; Sun). These cycles of negotiation are exhibited in multiple ways, evidenced through movements that take place on computer screens as well as in physical spaces while translators negotiate language with their bodies.

For example, in my second research site, the Language Services Department at the Hispanic Center of Western Michigan (discussed in chapter 6), Sara (a translator and the director of the office) moves words across the screen to test out various translation options, while simultaneously moving her fingers back and forth on her computer screen. During this process, Sara envisions various sentence structures and thinks about how these sentences will be perceived by Spanish-speaking readers, moving recursively, both in her writing and with her gesturing, to make sense of these translation options. In addition to the recursive practices of individual translators, translation processes within larger-scale projects undergo several writing and revision cycles, as a project moves from the initial quoting phase to proofreading and editing phases (Dimitrova). Throughout these processes, translators coordinate resources as they move recursively through digital platforms and material spaces, shifting from online dictionaries, to Spanish-language news sites such as Univision, to having a conversation with other translators in the office. These recursive practices are the rhetorical work embedded in translation—work often left invisible and often experienced only within the translation office. As I further demonstrate in my case studies, analyzing translation through this revised rhetoric model requires accounting for the recursivity embedded in language transformation and valuing the movement and coordination of digital and linguistic practices as critical to the success of culturally situated translation work.

Orienting to translation through cultural-rhetorical frameworks can help us understand the movement and the pauses in translation as part of the rhetorical labor embedded in these activities, rather than dismissing this work as a means to an end in language transformation. By understanding translation as a cyclical process, we can also see how translators' training and previous experiences may impact their approaches to and successes with specific translation projects.

Pillar 3: Translation is a ~~mechanical~~ creative act

In rhetoric and composition, technical communication, and related areas, the work of translation often remains hidden, visible only to the people engaged in translation activities (Maylath, Muñoz Martín, and Pacheco Pinto). For example, when texts and technologies are being developed for use with international, multilingual audiences, translation is frequently outsourced to translation professionals who "take care" of the language transformation, often without being given any authorship or intellectual credit (Batova and Clark; Walton, Zraly, and Mugengana). In classroom contexts, while we may acknowledge the "myth of linguistic homogeneity" (Matsuda) by recognizing that language diversity is a contemporary reality in all settings, we frequently ignore the translation work in which students are engaging as they make sense of our assignments, expectations, and assessment methods. In all of these cases, translation is positioned as an automated, mechanical activity that is separate from the creative, intellectual work of writing and communication. In other words, translation work is frequently deemed a tangential service to or a separate activity from the creative work embedded in content creation.

As the case studies in this book demonstrate, accurate and effective translations require highly creative, rhetorical work that is embedded at several parts of the translation process. For example, to navigate rhetorical choices during translation moments, translators have to manipulate and coordinate multiple modes simultaneously. In addition to manipulating language to fit the particular goals and interests of their specific communities, translators have to adapt and creatively navigate several digital platforms (Pym), leveraging their understanding of digital algorithms (e.g., those embedded in Google Translate) within their knowledge of language, culture, and community. In turn, as translators make decisions during translation moments, they make intellectual contributions to the information being disseminated across languages, as well as providing the labor needed to translate and redesign information for multilingual users.

To achieve accurate translations, multilingual communicators creatively layer and repurpose meaning, developing solutions to navigate translation moments so that meaning can be not only replaced but also accurately repurposed and localized across languages. Due to shifting cultural values and histories, linguistic elements like metaphors, jokes, and technical language frequently cannot be easily translated from one language to another (Newmark). Thus, to convey all linguistic elements and their implications across languages, translators engage in extensive creative and intellectual processes that require rhetorical negotiation and technical expertise. Analyzing translation through this revised orientation and paying attention to the specific ways through which translators navigate translation moments can help us better account for, understand, and leverage the creativity and rhetorical dexterity that drives successful language transformation. In addition, by acknowledging the creativity encompassed in translation, we can continue to recognize the intellectual labor in which students and professionals engage as they make sense of information in English-dominant contexts.

• A Revised Rhetoric of Translation gives us an orientation through which we can approach our analysis of translation moments in situated contexts. Through this framework, we can remain aware of both the visible and invisible elements influencing translation, noting the rhetorical work that is taking place as translators navigate various influences. In the chapters that follow, I use this reorientation to linguistic adaptation as I present examples of how translation was enacted at my two research sites. As I mention in chapter 2, I chose to study translation at these two particular sites for several reasons. First, I was interested in working with community-driven, Latinx translators who use their linguistic and cultural skills to provide language accessibility and to advocate for their communities. In addition, I chose to work with these two organizations due to the drastic differences in their work and objectives.

While both translators at Knightly Latino News (KLN) and those in the Language Services Department at the Hispanic Center of Western Michigan translate across Spanishes and Englishes for their communities, translation at KLN is driven mostly by student translators—undergraduate students enrolled in a public relations and communication program in a large public state university in central Florida. Although students at KLN have training in news broadcasting, they have no formal training in translation. Hence, their translation practices are driven primarily through their experiential learning, as they learn to adapt information into Spanish for a predominantly South American and Central American audience in Florida.

At my second research site, the Language Services Department, translators undergo different types of training focused on their specific area of interest. In this professional context, the term *translation* references the written adaptation of words across languages, while the term *interpretation* references verbal translation. Each translator or interpreter in the Language Services Department completes training workshops and works to attain national certification at several different levels. These certifications require them to pass examinations through national organizations such as the American Translators Association, the Certification Commission for Healthcare Interpreters, and the National Council on Interpreting in Healthcare, among many others. For this reason, the rhetorical strategies and the modes and modalities from which translators and interpreters draw to complete their work are based both on their individual experiences with language transformation and on the formal training that they complete as part of their job.

In chapters 5 and 6, I further describe the translation work taking place at KLN and in the Language Services Department, paying close attention to how translators in these organizations work simultaneously across modalities and languages to translate information. Enacting A Revised Rhetoric of Translation that accounts for different dimensions of language transformation, I use visuals, video montages, and narrative to provide a contextualized illustration of how translation moments are navigated in practice. In this way, I provide examples of specific translation moments, paying attention to how modalities and languages are deployed in situated contexts, and I also intricately describe the environments surrounding this translation work. Thus, in each chapter presenting a case study, I provide (1) an introduction to the specific research site in which I studied translation, noting the histories and lived experiences of the people involved in each organization; (2) a story of how I came to build relationships with the individuals at the research site, grounding this relationship as a critical component to my analytical framework; (3) specific examples of how multimodal elements are deployed in the translation moment activities of the translators at the research site; and (4) a more contextualized description of how this multimodal/multilingual work influences both the specific translators at the site and the surrounding community for whom the translation work is completed. By providing this context around translation and by intricately explaining the strategies developed and used to navigate translation moments in each situation, I continue to illustrate how translation encompasses practices useful for guiding how we theorize, research, and teach multimodal/multilingual communication.

5 • How Do Multilingual Students Navigate Translation?

Translation Moments at Knightly Latino News

Writing for Knightly Latino is not about writing in Spanish. It's not about writing in English. It's about living all the time in both worlds and knowing where to go in the moment.

—NATALIE, KNIGHTLY LATINO NEWS

Using the framework of A Revised Rhetoric of Translation discussed in chapter 4 and the analytical units of translation moments introduced in chapter 1, I here illustrate the multilingual and multimodal translation practices of student translators and bilingual news broadcasters at Knightly Latino News (KLN), a bilingual, student-run organization in news broadcasting, located at the University of Central Florida (UCF) in Orlando. Students in this organization create and translate news stories published on the student-run English network Knightly News from English to Spanish, for their Latinx community. To present the translation work that takes place at KLN, I first provide some background and contextual information about this organization and its student translators. I then share a story that illustrates the relationship building that made this collaboration possible. Finally, using the framework of A Revised Rhetoric of Translation, I further discuss multilingual/multimodal translation practices as they were enacted by student translators at KLN. I thread conversations in multilingual/multimodal communication through this discussion, highlighting how translation moments can inform the analysis of multilingual communicative practices.

Fig. 5. A student translator, Brigitte, working for Knightly Latino News

Background on KLN

I began working with KLN when I was introduced to the director of the organization, Katie Coronado, during my faculty orientation at UCF. Katie, an instructor at UCF and an immigrant from Cuba with decades of experience in the field of news broadcasting, started KLN because she wanted to give bilingual Latinx students at UCF the opportunity to work in both Spanish and English news networks. As a faculty member in the Nicholson School of Communication (where KLN is housed), Katie built this organization to help her students leverage their linguistic and cultural resources as they go into industry, where some have acquired jobs at Univision, Telemundo, and several other Latinx news networks.

One of the many things that inspired me to work with KLN is the location of the school that houses this program. UCF, where I earned my

BA and MA degrees before working as a full-time writing instructor from 2011 to 2013, is the second largest university (based on student population) in the United States. With over sixty thousand students, this university is home to thousands of students from all over the United States and abroad. Hosting a Latinx student population of 21.5 percent, UCF became listed by the federal government as a Hispanic-serving institution in 2016. Latinx students at UCF are primarily children of immigrant parents from South and Central America as well as children from Puerto Rican descent.

Together, Spanish-speaking UCF students represent dozens of different nations and language variations. In turn, to "speak Spanish" at UCF can mean a wide range of different things—different norms, variations, and levels of linguistic experience and expertise. Having learned a bit about the Latinx population at UCF through my previous experiences, I know that many of the Spanish-speaking students at UCF are full-time students with full-time employment outside of the university. In fact, all of the students working at KLN during my data collection period had other jobs and internships outside of the university (at news stations, banks, grocery stores, and restaurants) and were considered at least partial financial contributors to their households. Hence, for many of the students in this organization, the decision to volunteer for after-school activities is difficult, requiring them to manage already overwhelming work and school schedules.

I mention all of these factors to introduce KLN because context is important when considering the linguistic practices of any population. The translation work taking place at KLN is a product of cultural, economic, and social negotiation, as participants navigate their cultural and linguistic experiences while also juggling several academic and economic pressures. These factors all come into play in the translation process, when linguistic adaptations and the accuracy of these adaptations rely on the experiences and expertise of the translators and their communities of practice. Thus, translation work at KLN illustrates the three primary pillars of A Revised Rhetoric of Translation (explained in chapter 4), helping us understand translation as a situated practice that requires rhetorical movement across languages, modalities, and cultures.

I began formally collecting data with KLN in 2013, during the first year of my PhD program at Michigan State University. I was experiencing my own transitions as I adapted to life in Michigan, so visits to the KLN studio were a sort of homecoming for me. Because I grew up in similar ways to the students at KLN, my interactions with these participants were not founded on the typical participant-researcher binary. While I had not met any of my participants before collecting data for this project (since the students at KLN change every couple of years), forming relationships with these students was the most important and most rewarding aspect of this project.

To introduce translation at KLN, particularly through the framework of A Revised Rhetoric of Translation, I share the following excerpt from one of the journal entries I wrote after my initial meeting with KLN students during the fall of 2013. I wrote this entry on the plane ride home after the meeting, which was the first time I returned to UCF after moving to Michigan (hence the title of the entry, "Coming Home"). I present this entry both to introduce my participants at KLN and to provide some insights into the relationships that later fueled my methods and methodologies for working with this community.

This journal entry illustrates an early development of A Revised Rhetoric of Translation, showcasing how I came to understand the practice of translation as culturally situated (pillar 1), cyclical (pillar 2), and creative (pillar 3) and as best understood in situated rhetorical contexts. As you read the story, notice the discussions of language and brief linguistic shifts that take place (e.g., movements from English to Spanish) and how these shifts are prompted by other material factors (e.g., the comfort level among students and myself, the setup of the room, and the sharing of personal experiences). All of these elements ground the rhetorical work of translation and play critical roles in my analysis of translation moments with this organization.

Gonzales Journal Entry, 15 October 2013: "Coming Home"

I walked into the conference room where my first meeting with Knightly Latino students would take place, armed with bags full of snacks and an overly active mind that kept racing. I knew from the beginning that this place felt like home. As an immigrant from Bolivia who grew up in Florida, I know what it's like to commute to school every day after working long hours to support yourself and your family.

Unlike most other meetings I attend, I knew that my best prep for this meeting would be to simply sit and share—to listen to and tell stories. As I continued setting up, a young woman walked into the room, eyes tired but bright, smile shining at the sight of sandwiches, wearing a sweatshirt and flip-flops, with her hair put up in a bun ten seconds before leaving the house. I knew this girl, without introductions. I had been this girl, and in many ways, I'm still this girl (though flip-flops do not work in Michigan).

"Hi miss, are you the one here to talk to us?" she said.

"Yep, come on in and get some food. I'm Laura, by the way."

"I'm Ana. Hey do you need help moving the tables? I can help."

"Sure, thanks," I said, hoping she would be more spatially aware than I am and therefore able to make sense of how to best rearrange the tables in the room.

After Ana and I rearranged the room, got our sandwiches, and continued chatting, more students walked in the room—all smiling, all doubtful but welcoming, all tired and happy to see sandwiches.

Don't get me wrong, I had a PowerPoint (I always do), with maps, diagrams, and numbers. But as we sat around those oddly arranged desks and tables and looked at each other, a sense of comfort came over the room that I couldn't break by pulling up any slides.

We sat.

We ate sandwiches.

We introduced each other—not with the typical "My name is ——, and my major is ——," but, admittedly following my lead, with "My name is ——, and I'm here because ——."

"My name is Laura, and I'm here because I know you do cool things and I want to learn from you—also because it's warm here and because my heart is in Florida with UCF students."

"Hey, my name is Ana, and I'm here because it's my only day off work so I come to campus and do as much as I can."

"Hi, my name is Natalie, and I'm here because Katie told me you want to work with us and she said you're bringing lunch."

"Hola, me llamo Albert, and I'm here porque, ¿porque no? My friends are here."

"Well, thanks for coming. I really appreciate you taking the time out of what I know is a busy day to be here. Like Katie may have mentioned, I'm here because I'm hoping to work with you. Katie told me about the incredible work you do with Knightly Latino, and I would love to learn more about what you do for the group. But before I tell you about any of that, I want to tell you a long-winded story about why I'm really here. It's mostly because of a grudge I started to have in fifth grade.

"No, I'm serious. Fifth grade.

"In fifth grade, I was about to graduate from Bonneville Elementary School right down the road, by Lake Picket Road. Any of you go to Bonneville? Yeah? Guess I'm not that old yet.

"Anyway, in fifth grade, I asked my teacher, Ms. Weiss, to recommend me for advanced language arts in Middle School, partly because I had an A in English, but mostly because my best friends Michelle and Melissa were going into advanced language arts and I wanted to be in the same class as them. You know how it is in middle school—your friends are your lifeline.

Despite my current A in language arts, Ms. Weiss said she wouldn't recommend me for advanced language arts in middle school, because I was 'special.' She learned from her colleague, Ms. Dupuy, whom I had in third grade, that I had been in ESOL for two years before coming into her fifth-grade class. She told me that she learned English is not my first language and that advanced language arts is for people who learned English first.

On that day, I went home and told *mi papi* that Ms. Weiss said I couldn't go to advanced language arts in middle school, so I wasn't going to be in the class with Michelle and Melissa. I also told him that I didn't think it was fair—partly because nothing is fair when you're in fifth grade, but also because I thought my English could never be good enough if people kept knowing that I speak Spanish as my first language. I had to hide that. I told him, 'I have to hide my Spanish and pretend I don't know it. Then I can go to college and major in English and teach new students and tell them they don't have to speak English first to be advanced.' Yep, I was a pretty vengeful fifth grader. And not much has changed."

As Ana, Natalie, Albert, and the other students from Knightly Latino listened, I knew we were connecting. There were the familiar nods and *hmms* and *ughs* I typically hear from people who not only sympathize with my story but also relate to it—it's their story as much as it's mine.

"So when I tell you I'm here because of a grudge, I'm not lying," I continued.

"But also, as I'm sure you can imagine, Ms. Weiss isn't the only one I have a grudge against. I also hold a grudge against people who say students who speak languages other than English are less smart. I hold a grudge against the faculty members who complain about international or immigrant students' 'struggles' in the classroom. I hold a grudge against people who say we need 'help' to learn, when really they just need help to listen.

"I want to be a professor. They say it's a professor's job to 'build knowledge' about their very specific area of study. I'm here because I want to build knowledge about how smart, creative, and resourceful we are. But I'm not here to study you. I'm really here to listen to you and to share your ideas with others when, where, and *if* you think it might be useful."

We talked about methods. We talked about how to visualize translation through screencasts and about empirical methodologies commonly employed in writing studies and in technical communication. We talked about research as collaborative practice, and we decided to build knowledge together. This is the most exciting work I've ever done, with the best lessons I've ever learned.

As we continued planning what now (to my joy) became our project, one student, Janisa, looked up and said, "Yo quiero decir algo" (*I want to say something*)."

"You know how you were talking about ESOL? I just wanna say that I feel you. Like, when you say a grudge, I know what you mean. 'Cause, like, I was in ESOL in high school, and they would keep you in the same class as everyone else but then give you an extra thirty minutes or something on your tests. And it's nice and everything, and I would always take the extra thirty minutes to read, but I always thought I was stupid because everyone else would be done earlier. Then I got to college, and I'm not in ESOL, but I'm in these big classes. They take the thirty extra minutes away, but then a teacher will give everyone, like, four hours for a test, and everyone will still leave before me. I always take the whole four hours, and I still somehow feel stupid for taking longer than other people. Like, my grades are good, but I feel stupid because I was told the slow kids need the extra thirty minutes. So I'm like, am I taking more time because my English is still not good—like, is that what that means?"

As Janisa told this story, Natalie was nodding incessantly, saying, "Yeah, exactly. Yup." Then Natalie added, "You know, like, we're always questioning, Is my English 'good'? Is my Spanish 'good'? I don't know about y'all but when I write in Spanish, I use the dictionary and Google just as much if not more than when I write in English, 'cause I don't practice writing in Spanish that much. So I guess what I would wanna show in this project is that writing for Knightly Latino is not about writing in Spanish. It's not about writing in English. It's about living all the time in both worlds and knowing where to go in the moment, figuring out how you can say your ideas to the people you're trying to inform in the way that will be best for them, whatever it takes—English, Spanish, Spanglish, Google, whatever it takes to inform our people."

• Since the 2013 meeting described in the preceding journal entry, Natalie's comment regarding translation as a practice that requires multilingual communicators to live "in both [Spanish- and English-speaking] worlds" and to make rhetorical decisions about "where to go in the moment" using "whatever it takes" has resonated with me throughout my work both with KLN and with other community organizations that practice translation. This practice of moving "between worlds" while simultaneously transforming information across languages reflects all three pillars of A Revised Rhetoric of Translation, allowing us to see the rhetorical practices and situated elements of translation as cultural, cyclical, and creative activities that echo contemporary definitions of multilingual/multimodal communication. In the sections that follow, I provide specific examples of how multimodal elements are used in translation moments in the activities of the translators at KLN. In addition, I continue demonstrating that a multimodal analysis of translation moments allows us to understand how language transformation encompasses the deployment of visual, embodied, and digital elements.

Multimodality in Translation at KLN

As other scholars have noted (e.g., Ball, Arola, and Sheppard; Banks; McKee and DeVoss; Selfe; Shipka), multimodal composition, at least in contemporary models, is not about a specific tool or technology but about the importance and rhetorical ability to move between and across tools, technologies, and other semiotic resources and practices to make meaning for and with different audiences. Effective multimodal communication is not about mastering a particular digital platform but about figuring out which combination of platforms and tools within those platforms most successfully meets the needs of a particular audience at a particular moment in time. In essence, then, multimodal communication is about the ability to "go" where your audience needs you to "go in the moment," about figuring out how to help ideas move across "worlds" or contexts, and about using and leveraging the appropriate tools and technologies needed to make these transitions in situated instances.

A video montage is available (https://doi.org/10.3998/mpub.9952377. cmp.2) that serves as an additional introduction to how participants at KLN navigate among "worlds" (e.g., languages, technologies, and cultures) through their experiences translating news stories for their communities. As you watch the video, notice both what participants are saying and how their bodies are moving in their interactions with each other and with me as their interviewer. Note particularly how participants' body language shifts as they speak in Spanish, English, or a combination of the two languages (i.e., Spanglish). This video includes clips from several meetings that I recorded in the KLN office, as well as clips from artifact-based interviews with participants and with Katie, the director of KLN.

As evidenced in the video montage, translation at KLN is an everyday cultural practice—taking place at every meeting, every interaction, and every story and linking back to the individual histories of specific participants while simultaneously reflecting the identities and goals that tie the community together. In line with the first pillar of A Revised Rhetoric of Translation, the translation moments I encountered at KLN frequently led to culturally situated stories regarding participants' backgrounds and histories. For example, approximately twenty-six seconds into the introduction video mentioned above, a participant, Ana, discusses why she decided to pitch her story in English (rather than Spanish) during that day's meeting. As she explains her decision, Ana tells a story about her early experiences in elementary school, stating, "I was raised speaking Spanish, but the [education] system was designed to, instead of helping me embrace my first language, to tell me, 'No, we don't do that here. We don't speak that language here.'"

As she continues her story, Ana shares the internal dialogue that occurred when she thought of Spanish at a young age: "All I could hear is 'No, we don't do that here.'" When she would try to speak Spanish in her classroom or to use Spanish when words in English were not readily available, Ana's teachers would reprimand her, telling her, "No, that language is not acceptable here." For this reason, now that she is in college, she does not feel as comfortable communicating in Spanish as she does in English, primarily because she worked so hard as a child to "get rid of" her Spanish use.

Translation moments such as the ones exhibited by Ana took place repeatedly during the KLN meetings I attended. As KLN members share knowledge with each other and plan for future events as a community, they have to consider not only which languages will be comfortable for their audiences but also which languages the translators themselves feel confident using. As Juan Guerra explains ("Cultivating"), the movement between languages is a rhetorical choice for multilingual speakers, one that is often influenced by cultural histories and power structures. For some students, losing confidence in their heritage languages comes as a result of the educational system that they experienced, one that consistently favors the use of normed standardized American English. Now that the movement between languages is more accepted within mainstream US classrooms, students like Ana are struggling to implement their heritage languages into their practices. Although programs like KLN encourage and even require the use of Spanish, some students who have spent many years in English-dominant spaces struggle to regain expertise in their heritage languages. This causes them to experience more translation moments, both as they translate from their heritage languages into English and vice versa.

In another translation moment exhibited in my introduction video, Katie, the director of KLN, discusses the purposes and history of KLN, during an interview with me. At about 0:52 in the video, Katie pauses as she begins to think about how to answer the question "What is your goal for students working at KLN?" During this pause, which lasts from 0:55 to 1:05, Katie stays silent, trying to figure out how to word her answer. At approximately 1:06, Katie admits, "I think I'm thinking in Spanish." At this point, I tell her, "You can talk in Spanish," and Katie's face brightens up. Her eyebrows move up, and she excitedly says, "I can? Ok." No more than three seconds later, Katie goes on to give an elaborate response to my interview question, explaining how KLN provides opportunities for students to connect with both Spanish-speaking and English-speaking audiences across the world.

Figure 6 presents a multimodal time map with images illustrating still shots from approximately one minute of the video's interaction between Katie and myself, where Katie initially struggles to answer my question in English, realizes she can answer in Spanish, and then continues to provide her response. The figure allows us to pay close attention to the transitions Katie was experiencing during this brief translation moment. In the beginning frame on the left-hand side, Katie's lips are scrunched and her eyes are looking up, as she deliberates an approach to my question. The second frame shows the moment after Katie reluctantly admits, "I think I'm thinking in Spanish." You can almost see shame in her face; her eyes turn, and her teeth become slightly exposed as she gently grinds them. After I say, "You can talk in Spanish," Katie's face lights up, her eyebrows lifting and her eyes broadening, as shown in the third frame of figure 6. In the fourth frame, Katie takes a moment to collect her thoughts, her lips coming together to frame her pensive expression. Lastly, as evidenced in the video clip and in the last frame of figure 6, Katie moves her shoulders to help her sit up straight, as she looks directly into the camera and begins to speak in a fluent, confident Spanish, explaining exactly what she could not express in English alone. In this way, for the last remaining seconds of this interaction, Katie speaks consistently, using broad hand gestures and looking confidently at me (her audience), as she proudly describes the work of KLN.

For Katie, negotiating the translation moment illustrated in figure 6 encompassed multimodal interactions in that it required the layering of

00:52

"Hmm...I'm thinking in Spanish..."

"I can talk in Spanish?!"

"Ok so..."

1:55

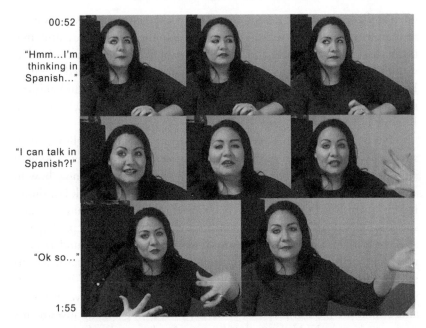

Fig. 6. Katie Coronado, director of KLN, moving from English to Spanish during an interview

linguistic codes in both Spanish and English. To answer my question about her goal for students working at KLN, Katie had to decide on an answer in her mind and then decide how she could present the answer to me as her audience. Much like many academic spaces in the United States, Katie initially perceived this interaction to be limited to the constraints of the English language, causing Katie to pause and momentarily lose confidence in her answer, perhaps recalling previous experiences of being shamed when using Spanish, in the same way that her students recall these experiences during the conversations depicted in the introduction video.

Upon being told that this interaction was not constrained to English alone, however, Katie was able to eloquently present her answer, using multimodal resources (in this case, through her confident stance and hand gestures) to firmly make a case for the value of KLN and the future of her students. In this case, multimodal elements were brought into Katie's translation moment, both through her gesturing and through her movement between English and Spanish. Throughout the entire interaction, the way that Katie used language and the rhetorical choices she made in her language use were tied both to her own cultural background and to her goals as the leader and representative of the KLN community. Katie wanted to represent herself and her language abilities in the video while simultaneously discussing the goals and motivations of KLN as a whole. Understanding Katie's response to my question required acknowledgment of Katie's linguistic strengths as well as of her linguistic history and culture-specific experiences as an immigrant in the United States who learned English as a second language.

Like many multilingual students who do not identify English as their strongest language for every rhetorical situation, Katie was never lacking in an answer to my question. Indeed, she did not say, "I don't know how to answer that question," but instead reluctantly admitted, "I think I'm thinking in Spanish." The distinction between thinking in one language and speaking or writing in another language was common among all participants at KLN, perhaps signaling the rhetorical work that individuals undertake as they translate their ideas across modes and modalities. In this particular instance, without making the assertion "You can talk in Spanish" in our conversation, I could have very easily assumed that Katie did not have an answer and/or that she was not prepared to describe her own goals and investments in the students at KLN. Instead, Katie was simply experiencing some hesitance to translating her ideas successfully, even though these ideas were effectively crafted and presented in Spanish. For this reason, as we continue enacting A Revised Rhetoric of Translation, linking linguistic diversity to culture and history, it is important to open up the possibility for composing in our classrooms and workplaces by emphasizing the fact that, should they choose to, students and professionals can both think and communicate in codes and languages outside of the normed SWE.

Rather than assuming that students and professionals cannot answer our questions, we should remain open to the possibility that students are merely answering questions in a language other than English, and we should make space for these rhetorical practices whenever possible (Guerra, "Cultivating"; Williams and Pimentel). Our communicative practices are never separate from our cultural histories and our lived experiences, and the motivation for communication can often be tied back to our communities of practice, particularly for multilingual communities of color who fight adversity to move forward in the English-dominant United States (Williams and Pimentel). Understanding translation practices (and composing practices more broadly) through the first pillar of A Revised Rhetoric of Translation (both at KLN and in other spaces) can help us intentionally link verbal and written acts of communication to invisible and perhaps seemingly irrelevant cultural/linguistic experiences.

In addition to multimodal translation experiences that echo KLN's cultural makeup, participants at KLN layered other multimodal communicative practices to translate news stories for their community. Analyzing the translation moments that KLN participants experienced in digital spaces, in particular, helped me further understand the cyclical, creative rhetorical work that is at play as multilingual communicators negotiate meaning during translation moments. This understanding aligns with the second and third pillars of A Revised Rhetoric of Translation.

Digitally Mediated Multimodality at KLN

During my time working with student translators at KLN, I asked several participants to use Camtasia Relay, a screencast recording software, to record their computer screens as they worked on story translations for KLN. Two of the KLN participants, Natalie and Brigitte, consistently submitted screencast recordings of their work throughout the duration of the project. As they submitted screencast recordings of their translation processes, I coded and analyzed their practices and conducted artifact-based interviews with the participants to further understand their reasoning and motivation for completing translation activities. During these interviews, I would meet individually with either Natalie or Brigitte and play clips from their screencast recordings, asking whether they were doing what I thought they were or if they could tell me more about what they were using to translate a specific word or phrase in a specific story. By conducting artifact-based interviews with participants throughout my coding process, I was able to triangulate my analysis with my participants' own interpretations of the data. Through these collaborative efforts, I was able to draw some conclusions about how Natalie and Brigitte moved simultaneously across languages and technologies to rhetorically and creatively translate news stories for KLN.

Brigitte's Translation Practices: Using Resources to "Get a Start"

When I first met Brigitte, she had been working at KLN for less than one semester. An immigrant from Venezuela, Brigitte moved to Florida with her family when she was in elementary school. She first learned to speak English there. After years of working to "perfect" her English, Brigitte actually felt more comfortable writing and speaking in English in her daily interactions once she was of college age. However, because Spanish is really important to Brigitte, she enrolled in KLN as a way to practice her heritage language and to gain experience that would help her become a bilingual news broadcaster.

During one of our early interviews, Brigitte described her translation practices by stating, "Since I'm new to translating, I'm not always sure how to start the translation. I use Google Translate to get a start. Once I see the word choices, I can fix them to sound better, but it's hard for me to come up with the words at first." Brigitte's claim that she "fixes" the translation options provided by Google Translate is evident in the screencast recordings of her translation process. In figure 7, I provide a visualization of a typical translation sequence for Brigitte, illustrating how she uses Google Translate as a site of invention when navigating translation moments. In the key provided on the right-hand side of the image, I provide icons to represent three different strategies I found in my coding of the translation moments I analyzed at KLN. These coding strategies include the use of digital translation tools (e.g., Google Translate); negotiating, which was coded as any instance when translators were debating between several possible translation options (e.g., asking, "Should I use this word or that word?"); and deconstructing, which took place when translators conjugated or broke down words in their translation to grammatically fit within the sentences they were writing across languages.

Figure 7 visualizes three translation moments that Brigitte experienced when translating a news story from English to Spanish. During this sequence, Brigitte was translating a news article related to student loan debt in the United States and its potential impact on the US economy. Specifically, she was working on translating the sentence "The increase in student loan subsidies will be an investment that will lead to economic growth." Rather than breaking the sentence apart or translating it in pieces, Brigitte began by translating a set of words and phrases in the sentence, before typing any translation. As figure 7 illustrates, Brigitte put the words *investment* and *increase* and the phrase "will lead to economic growth" into Google Translate right away and then used the first definition provided through this digital translation tool in her translation. However, after looking up the initial sequence of words and phrases in Google Translate, Brigitte used negotiation strategies (making decisions between word options) and deconstruction strategies (conjugating words or phrases to fit within the translated sentence) to present a final translation of the entire sentence. For instance, rather than using the word *aumentar* as the translation of *increase*, Brigitte deconstructed the word into *aumento* in her final translation.

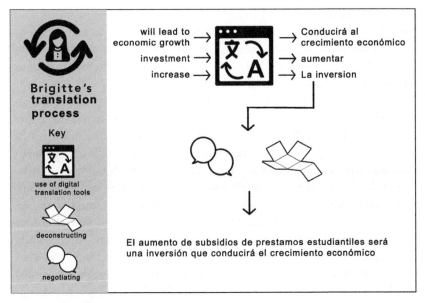

Fig. 7. Visualization of the translation process of KLN student translator Brigitte

During her artifact-based interview, Brigitte watched her screencast recording and explained, "I use Google Translate to translate all the parts of a sentence that I'm having trouble with first, because I have a hard time coming up with the words I want to use in Spanish." Although Brigitte could not think of the translation for the word *increase* initially, once the word *aumentar* was provided by Google Translate, Brigitte did know how to adequately conjugate and deconstruct the word to accurately fit her translated sentence. Hence, Brigitte explains, "Once I see the word, I know how to fix it to fit what I'm trying to say, but since I'm used to talking in English most of the time at school, I have a hard time coming up with the words at first." In this example, Brigitte used Google Translate as a form of invention, getting and adapting definitions to fit the context of her writing. When she could not think of a specific word in her translation, Google Translate served as a site of creativity and innovation for Brigitte, one that would prompt and launch her ideas.

During another translation moment, Brigitte translated an article regarding a new building in downtown Orlando. The article referenced tensions between the popular tourist appeal of International Drive (an area of town that hosts many theme parks and tourist attractions) and the more locally recognized venues located in downtown Orlando. Similar to the process depicted in figure 7, Brigitte began by putting several words and phrases into Google Translate, including *downtown*, *city*, and *building*. Rather than using the first translations provided for all words put into Google Translate, however, Brigitte further negotiated these translations through the use of other digital and rhetorical resources.

Google translated *downtown* to the Spanish phrase "centro de la ciudad," which is a literal translation meaning "center of the city." During her interview, Brigitte explained that she did not want to use that more formal phrase, because "people who live in Orlando wouldn't talk about downtown like that, like center of the city." Dissatisfied with Google's translation of the word *downtown*, Brigitte went to Telemundo's website, a bilingual Spanish/English news network. Using that site's search bar, she searched for "downtown Orlando" on the site and found several entries that referenced "Orlando" without referencing downtown. After visiting Telemundo's website, Brigitte went back to her article and used the word *Orlando* without referencing downtown. She omitted Google's suggested phrase, "centro de la ciudad," and instead used *Orlando* to reference downtown Orlando and used "la international drive en Orlando" to reference the tourist area described in the English article.

During her interview, Brigitte described her negotiation process in translating the references to "downtown Orlando": "A lot of times, I'll Google a word if I have no idea how to use it, and I'll look up the word on Telemundo or Univision, just to get some context clues for how it's used in the media." After looking up the word *downtown* on Google Translate, Brigitte had enough rhetorical knowledge to understand that the Latinx community in Orlando would not use the formal phrase "centro de la ciudad" to reference their city. Additionally, Brigitte knew to leverage other digital resources by visiting bilingual news sites that would be familiar to her intended audience, using articles from the websites for Telemundo or Univision (another Spanish/English news station) as a reference point for her translations. Thus, Brigitte ensured that her final translation would be not only literally accurate (as the phrase "centro de la ciudad" would be) but also culturally localized to the Orlando Latinx community she aimed to reach.

As these brief examples illustrate, Brigitte's digital translation practices required that she find not only accurate representations of words and phrases across languages but also culturally appropriate language substitutions that met the needs of her intended audience. As a bilingual speaker who lives in Orlando, Brigitte knew how to coordinate digital, bilingual resources to come up with a translation that is both accurate and culturally appropriate, even if she at first felt as though she could not come up with the words to translate. In this way, Brigitte's movement across digital platforms, including Google Translate and the Telemundo and Univision websites, rendered a cyclical, recursive translation process that encompassed rhetorical composing across languages and platforms.

Brigitte's translation was never based on a linear, input/output model but instead required Brigitte to go back and forth between digital resources as she decided how to culturally localize translations to accurately meet the needs of her community. Although Brigitte was translating using traditional word-processing software (i.e., Microsoft Word), her digital coordination practices revealed a multimodal orientation to composing that echoes Shipka's call for teachers and researchers to pay attention to both multimodal products and multimodal production (*Toward a Composition*). To reach accurate translations, Brigitte had to navigate between digital platforms, going back and forth between the Word document that she was writing and the multiple sites (i.e., Google Translate, Telemundo, and Univision) that helped her make rhetorical decisions throughout her translation process. Although much of the digital coordination work that Brigitte was doing may have remained invisible from the final translation that she submitted, using screencast recordings in correlation with artifact-based interviews allowed me to more intricately trace the rhetorical work embedded in the translation moments that Brigitte experienced.

Natalie's Translation Practices: Figuring Out "Where to Go in the Moment"

As the student leader for KLN, Natalie had been translating stories for the organization for three years when we began working together on this project. During one of her initial interviews, she explained that she joined KLN because she wanted to get experience producing news stories in Spanish. As an advertising and public relations major, Natalie understood the importance of reaching the Latinx population in Florida. "Latinos *are* Florida," she explained during her interview, adding, "You can't say you are talking to Floridians if you're only producing news in English."

After being born in the Dominican Republic, Natalie moved to Orlando with her family at the start of middle school (sixth grade). While in the Dominican Republic, she had learned to speak Spanish first, but she had started to learn English even before her family moved to Florida. "To my family," Natalie stated, "both languages [Spanish and English] have always been important, because our family lives in both places [the Dominican Republic and Florida]."

Natalie's translation practices reflect her keen ability to seamlessly move between English and Spanish, valuing both languages and understanding the cultural implications of each language for specific communities. Like Brigitte, Natalie frequently used a digital translation tool, Google Translate, as a starting point for her translation. At the same time, she often layered deconstruction and negotiation strategies with the results she received from Google Translate. In this way, Natalie contextualized the translations provided by Google Translate, to address her audience more effectively. Figure 8 illustrates a typical translation moment for Natalie, where she layers the use of digital translation tools with negotiation and deconstruction strategies.

In the translation moment illustrated in figure 8, Natalie was translating the word *threaten* as it appeared in the story title "Development Plan Threatens Orlando Park." Natalie first put the word *threaten* into Google Translate, and Google provided four translation options: the word *amenazar*, the phrase "proferir amenazas contra," and the words *acechar* and *amagar*. All of these options were identified by Google Translate as synonymous to the English word *threaten*. Rather than using any of the initial options provided by Google Translate, however, Natalie searched for Spanish translations of the English word *harm*. Google Translate provided nine options for this translation, and Natalie decided to use the first option, the word *daño*, in her final translation. After negotiating between the word *threaten* and the word *harm*, Natalie deconstructed the word *daño* by conjugating it to fit grammatically into the article's title. She then decided to go with the word *daña* as her final translation.

During her artifact-based interview, Natalie explained why she did not use any of the initial suggestions provided by Google Translate: "The word *threaten* seemed to be translated into something more related to physical harm. If I 'amenazar' someone, for example, I'm threatening them physically. Threatening a park is completely different, because we are talking about an object and not a person, so I decided to look up options for the word *harm*, because I thought that might give me results that are more like harming a physical object instead of a human." As she negotiated between the implications of the words *amenazar* and *daño*, Natalie also negotiated her cultural understanding of both English and Spanish. In turn, Natalie localized the translations provided by Google Translate to better fit her intended audience, navigating between the digital translation tool and her

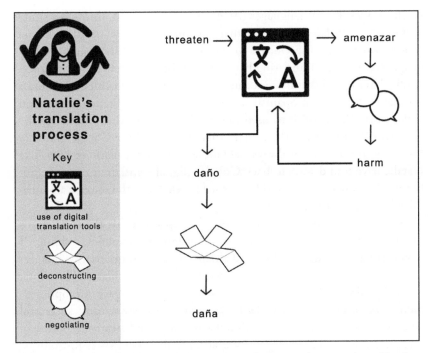

Fig. 8. Visualization of the translation process of KLN student translator Natalie

own cultural knowledge to make a rhetorical decision in her translation.

It is interesting that after realizing that the word *threaten* was translated by Google to *amenazar* and deciding that word was not appropriate for her context, Natalie decided to put another English word, *harm*, into Google Translate. Rather than searching for Spanish synonyms for *amenazar*, Natalie knew enough about the functionality of digital translation tools to select another word in English to help with her translation. During her artifact-based interview, Natalie explained why she looked up a second word in English (i.e., *harm*) rather than searching for Spanish synonyms: "The online tools are always better if you look something up in English. If you look something up in Spanish on Google, it won't be as accurate as if you can look it up English." Indeed, through this example, Natalie exhibits technical knowledge that aligns with current research regarding the state of digital translation tools. As explained by Chen and Bao and by Balk et al., digital translation tools in general and Google Translate in particular are guided by English-centered algorithms.

Although Google Translate now has capabilities to translate between seventy-two different languages (Arce), Balk et al. found, through a study of Google Translate's accuracy, that the most accurate translations are yielded when users use Google to translate from English to another language. Rather than translating between Spanish and French, for instance, studies have found that more accurate translations are provided when users translate a word from Spanish to English, English to French, and so on (ElShiekh). The algorithms used to organize Google's dictionaries are developed with English at the center. Therefore, searching Google Translate for words in English will always yield more accurate translations. Users like Natalie have found ways to hack Google's digital translation tool by combining their own cultural and linguistic knowledge with Google's algorithmically designed dictionaries.

As Natalie continued her interview, she explained that the translations provided by Google Translate "are just inspiration sometimes," adding, "I wouldn't have thought of the word *dañar* on my own necessarily, but seeing that *amenazar* was an option helped me think of similar words to look up in Spanish and English. The Google translations gave me options." Hence, as Natalie explains, digital translation tools are most successful when they are paired with the cultural knowledge and creative expertise of human users. The use of digital translation tools encompasses just one aspect of participants' multimodal translation practices, those that combine cultural and technological skills to transform information across languages.

As evidenced through Natalie's example, using the translations provided by Google Translate requires that users incorporate linguistic and cultural knowledge in two languages—in the case of Natalie's example, both Spanish and English. For Natalie, Google Translate served as a tool to help her own abilities to move between languages. Once multilingual communicators like Natalie find inspiration in digital translation tools or other digital platforms, they layer additional rhetorical strategies (e.g., deconstructing and negotiating) to come up with final translation versions representing cultural and linguistic knowledge that can be understood by specific communities. Thus, as multilingual communicators navigate digital platforms to translate, they creatively repurpose language to meet the specific needs and orientations of culturally specific audiences, continuing to reflect the three pillars of A Revised Rhetoric of Translation through multilingual/multimodal composing processes that are rhetorically and culturally situated.

• As KLN participants illustrate, translation is often accomplished via multiple, layered, and sequenced strategies that require a fluidity among languages and modalities (both material and embodied). It is very rare for a translator to only use one strategy or mode during the process of language transformation. Instead, translators like Natalie and Brigitte exemplify the complex negotiations of history, culture, and language that takes place as users translate words and phrases into English and/or Spanish. Those negotiations are most accurately completed by human translators who have enough experience and context to situate information across languages. Any single language, tool, or mode has its limitations in translation practices. Multilingual communicators like the ones depicted in this chapter make rhetorical decisions and work across communication spaces to reach translations that are both accurate and representative of both the source and the target languages that play a role in the story or the information being presented.

Through the negotiation of words like *downtown* and *threaten*, translators at KLN revealed the benefits of cultural knowledge to the translation process. In their navigation of translation moments, participants like Natalie and Brigitte were focused more on conveying experiences (e.g., emotions about downtown Orlando) than on providing "objective" or literal definitions of the translated words. While digital translation tools like Google Translate provide several translation options that are deemed grammatically accurate by machine algorithms, successfully negotiating translation moments requires that multilingual communicators move beyond precise or dictionary-based definitions and translations for specific terminology, privileging language variations and combinations that resonate most directly with the target population being addressed in specific interactions or contexts.

Translators like the ones at KLN have to exhibit the creative rhetorical dexterity required to successfully navigate the tools of multimodal communication. Although translators do not always know how to use all terminology in every language (just like multimodal composers do not know how to use every tool, modality, or technology), successful translation hinges on the rhetorical ability of multilingual communicators who coordinate the semiotic resources at their disposal to transform information in ways that most directly meet the needs of their particular audiences in specific moments in time. As Natalie, Brigitte, and other KLN participants illustrate, translation software and other digital tools and platforms are not places where multilingual communicators go for answers in the translation process; rather, these digital resources function as one portion in a bigger network of language and cultural practices that allow communicators to make rhetorical decisions during translation. Hence, translation tools and other digital platforms are sites for creativity and invention rather than for machine-automated answers, providing additional resources to accurately and successfully transform language. While these digital technologies are useful, I have found, after analyzing thousands of translation projects across two research sites, that digital platforms and translation software remain insufficient and inaccurate if they are not paired with the creative rhetorical ability of multilingual communicators who can manipulate language and technology simultaneously. Without Natalie's understanding of the algorithms embedded in digital translation software and without her creative manipulation of those algorithms as she chose what words to put into Google Translate, the translation work at KLN would not be as successful or culturally situated.

Student translators like Natalie and Brigitte (as well as the participants showcased in the video montage that frames this chapter) are critically aware of their roles as communicators who have to constantly move between audiences to share their ideas. Sticking to one language and/or one mode is not an option for translators at KLN, as they have to consider how the translation options presented to them by specific experiences and digital platforms would be interpreted by various audiences. It is important to note how lived experiences and histories influence the translation strategies enacted by multilingual communicators. For example, Brigitte's relatively new role at KLN caused her to experience several translation moments really early in her translation process. As evidenced in figure 7, Brigitte often put several words and phrases into Google Translate at the beginning of her translation sequence, using these initial options as "inspiration" for the rest of her process. Although Natalie also used Google Translate to get inspiration for her translation, her extended experience working at KLN and now heading the organization led her to focus on fewer (but more extended) translation moments. For instance, where Brigitte started her translation by putting three sets of words and phrases into Google Translate right away, Natalie put a single word, *threaten*, into Google Translate, taking more time to think through one single-word translation than Brigitte took in deconstructing and negotiating among her three initial translation moments.

As evidenced in the video montage discussed early in this chapter, KLN translators discussing news stories and potential translations often relive and retell stories they have experienced as bilingual immigrants living in the United States. The experiences that multilingual communicators have as they learn new languages, particularly when they are learning these languages in a new country, constantly influence how they engage in new communicative contexts. Like Katie's hesitation to speak Spanish during her interview, multilingual communicators may sometimes exhibit hesitancies to blending languages in their daily communication, not necessarily because they are not proficient or capable of using their linguistic resources, but because previous experiences have shown them that despite any recent efforts to pluralize language use in US contexts, all of our linguistic resources have not, in fact, historically been welcomed or accepted in traditionally English-dominant spaces (e.g., US classrooms and workplaces). Thus, it is important to note that the composing and communicative practices that we see in our classrooms and workplaces, particularly from multilingual communicators, do not always reflect the actual extent of the communicative potential present in these spaces. For example, multilingual communicators' pauses as they translate information in their minds do not necessarily indicate that they are incapable of answering or contributing to the conversations at hand. Understanding language practices through A Revised Rhetoric of Translation and acknowledging the rhetorical work of multilingual communicators pushes us to expand the ways in which we listen to and for language difference, so that we can understand pauses in translation as rhetorical work rather than as communicative deficits.

The work of student translators at KLN provided some insights into the rhetorical negotiations that take place during the translation processes of multilingual communicators. In particular, the analysis of translation at KLN allowed me to trace some connections between various multimodal elements embedded in translation, including the use of digital translation tools as well as the links between digital translation and lived experiences. Further, analyzing the translation practices of translators with different levels of experience in translation, such as Natalie and Brigitte, allowed me to trace some connection between how translators' level of comfort and expertise with the profession of translation may impact their coordination of modalities and technologies to transform language. In the following chapter, I extend on these connections between translators' professional training experiences and their approaches to navigating translation moments. Introducing the work of professional translators working in the Language Services Department at the Hispanic Center of Western Michigan, I highlight how translation in professional contexts embodies intricate, multimodal communication with high-impact exigencies and consequences.

6 • How Do Multilingual Professionals Translate?

Translation Moments in the Language Services Department at the Hispanic Center of Western Michigan

Los lenguajes están VIVOS—Languages are alive. Language moves, it breathes, it changes, and as translators we have to know how to adapt with it. That's a lot of work, and we have to do it every single day, in every single moment.

—SARA PROAÑO, DIRECTOR OF LANGUAGE SERVICES

After working with student translators at KLN, I wanted to further understand how the extent of translators' experiences and training influences their approach and engagement with language transformation. Because the translators introduced in chapter 5 did not necessarily have formal training in translation and represented a traditional college-age demographic, I deemed it important to connect with another community that may help me contextualize how translation activities play out in a professional setting. As Terese Guinsatao Monberg explains, when analyzing cultural-rhetorical work in context, it is important to acknowledge how individuals experience and navigate communication "*within* their own borders or communities," noting how individuals who may speak similar languages navigate their own "recursive spatial movement" as they make linguistic transitions (22; emphasis in original). In other words, even though translators at both of my research sites were moving between Spanishes and Englishes, it was important for me to work with two different organizations with different participants, so that I could more intricately understand how translation differences play out within distinct Spanish-speaking communities.

To understand how translation is enacted in professional contexts, I began working with employees in the Language Services Department at the Hispanic Center of Western Michigan, a small translation and interpretation office in Grand Rapids. In this chapter, I illustrate how professional translators navigate translation moments within this office, as they facilitate communication between Spanish-speaking community members and English-speaking service providers such as health care practitioners, government officials, and other local organizations. To introduce translation in this professional context, I first share some background information on the Language Services Department and the nonprofit organization that houses that establishment. As I did for KLN in chapter 5, I then share a narrative story that contextualizes the relationships I built with translators in the department. Finally, I provide specific examples of the multilingual/multimodal translation processes enacted by translators in the department, paying specific attention to the different ways in which professionals' translation activities inform A Revised Rhetoric of Translation. I end this chapter by emphasizing that translation in a professional context, particularly within the Language Services Department, is prompted by extreme exigencies for services and support and frequently results in powerful consequences for the livelihood of community members from historically marginalized backgrounds.

Background on the Language Services Department

The Hispanic Center of Western Michigan is a nonprofit organization located in Grand Rapids. The purpose of this organization is to provide access, education, and resources to the Latinx community in western Michigan and beyond (www.hispanic-center.org). Although the center as a whole is a nonprofit organization, the Language Services Department located inside the center is a for-profit translation and interpretation business aiming to provide language accessibility to the Latinx community. All of the revenue earned in the Language Services Department is reinvested in the Hispanic Center, fueling various programs for the larger organization (e.g., support groups for survivors of domestic violence, local youth initiatives, and campaigns concerned with Latinx health and wellness). In this way, the Language Services Department at the Hispanic Center works under the same institutional constraints as a nonprofit organization, while simultaneously charging a small service fee that is then reinvested into the community.

The Language Services Department at the Hispanic Center employs approximately thirty multilingual translators and interpreters, with verbal and written proficiency in Spanish, English, and a wide range of indigenous languages from South America, Central America, and North America. These professionals facilitate communication between, on the one hand, community members who identify with heritage languages other than English and, on the other, over fifty local service and government organizations in the city of Grand Rapids (e.g., the local police department, hospitals, Child Protective Services, technology businesses, local museums, and other nonprofit organizations). All of the interpreters and translators who work in the Language Services Department are trained in-house, meaning that the department recruits and trains multilingual community members from the Grand Rapids area who are interested in becoming professional translators and interpreters. Each year, the director of the Language Services Department, Sara Proaño, facilitates training programs that give bilingual or multilingual community members the hands-on training and experience needed to eventually be hired (either by the Language Services Department or by other local agencies) as interpreters and translators for the community. All of the interpreters and translators who work in the Language Services Department live in the community that they serve, gaining an income and supporting their families through the revenue earned by providing language accessibility to that same community.

Sara Proaño is a bilingual (Spanish- and English-speaking) professional translator and interpreter who holds a degree in neuropsychology from a university in Quito, Peru. She had been working at the Hispanic Center for approximately seven years at the start of my study. After immigrating from Peru and finding herself unemployed in the United States, Sara began working at the Hispanic Center by shredding papers and conducting other office duties, before moving up to direct the Language Services Department. Through her experiences rebuilding her career, Sara established and sustains what she describes as a "three-tiered approach to community engagement," one that fuels the foundation for the translation and interpretation work that takes place in the Language Services Department. During an interview with Sara, she defined her three-tiered approach through the following organizational goals:

1. language accessibility, which entails providing translation and interpretation services that allow Spanish-speaking community members to access social services and to adequately understand government procedures;

Fig. 9. Director Sara Proaño gesturing as she discusses translation in the Language Services Department

2. sustainability, which Sara defines as earning a modest income from language services and then applying that income to other initiatives within the Hispanic Center;
3. leadership and professional development, which includes providing workshops, training, and access to national certification exams for all translators and interpreters who work in the Language Services Department.

I spent two years forming relationships and collaborating with participants in the Language Services Department. During this time, I recorded over two thousand translation projects, both using screencast software to record how employees completed written translations on their computers and using video recordings to capture how participants interacted with each other and with their surrounding environment throughout their translation and interpretation activities. While collecting this data, I worked part-time in the Language Services Department, where I coordinated and completed various translation projects. Similar to my work at KLN, I conducted artifact-based interviews with employees at this research site, using these interviews as a way to triangulate my coding and analysis processes with my participants' own interpretations of their work. Although I will share specific examples of how translators in the Language Services Department enact multilingual/multimodal communication through their daily activities, I want to frame these examples through A Revised Rhetoric of Translation, specifically by sharing a story that illustrates how linguistic transformations are embedded in other rhetorical and cultural contexts within this organization. The following excerpts from my journal entries recording my first interactions with Sara in the Language Services Department illustrate how her leadership and vision shape the translation work in her department, while simultaneously influencing the well-being of the surrounding community.

Gonzales Journal Entry, 12 March 2014

Today was my first official day of work as the translations coordinator in the Language Services Department. Although I was a bit hesitant to come on board as a part-time employee while also collecting data for my dissertation, I will never forget Sara's words to me during our initial visit: "You can't just study translation without doing translation, Laura. I would love to have you here in the department. But if you want to be a part of us, you'll have to truly *be* a part of us."

At first, I didn't quite understand what Sara meant by "*be* a part of us." I thought that *not* working as an employee while studying the work of the office would allow me more time for reflection and analysis. However, what I've come to realize in just a few hours is that the driving force behind professional translation is the immediate exigence for and urgency of this work—an exigence that can't be described or understood through observation alone. Today, as I learned how to navigate the document templates housed on the department's computer, clients continuously walked through the door. Through this movement, each project in the office quickly became a person, a story in transition that needed my assistance—a mother seeking the translation of her children's vaccination records from Oaxaca so that she can enroll them in school, a hospital calling for an emergency interpretation to help during a surgery procedure, a young man coming through the door in need of a resume translation to help him find employment after his recent arrival in the US, a representative from the local morgue coming in twenty minutes before closing to request the translation of ten death certificates that needed to be delivered to families as soon as possible.

While I know that I would be sympathizing with all these stories if I were merely sitting in the corner of the room taking notes and video recording, the fact that it is now my job to coordinate these translation projects—figuring out which ones I can take care of myself in-house and which will need to be outsourced to other translators—completely reorients my approach to this work. These are no longer my participants, and this is no longer just my dissertation—this is my job in this community, and I now understand that what Sara was pushing me to do by requiring that I come on board as a translator was not just to help me with my project but to also ensure a reciprocal collaborative relationship that would allow me to contribute my language skills to the very community that would fuel my research. I have never been more grateful.

Gonzales Journal Entry, 24 March 2014

Today was my third Friday of work at the office. At the beginning of the day (after I got here late again!), Sara mentioned that she wanted to take me out to lunch. Because I don't live in Grand Rapids and I commute from Lansing each day, I haven't gotten the chance to see much of this town. Although I was super-excited, I couldn't quite wrap my head around how both Sara and I would be able to leave the office on a busy Friday to go have lunch. There's just always so much work to do.

At around 12:30, Sara closed her computer, pulled out her curling iron from inside a filing cabinet, and began curling her hair. She then handed me her lip gloss as I sat slouched over my computer: "Este color te va quedar bien. Esto es parte del trabajo, amiga" (*This color will look nice on you. This is part of the job, my friend*). A few minutes later, we walked out the door as Sara very politely informed Olga (the woman at the front desk), "Ya venimos. ¿Te traemos algo Olguita?" (*We'll be right back. Should we bring something back for you, Olguita?*). Sara is never the person to eat without offering to share. She reminds me of my *mami* that way.

As we walked out of our building and began walking through the neighborhood, Sara's shining smile greeted everyone who walked by us. Sometimes she would stop and wave, and other sometimes she would share a casual "Buen día!" (*Good day!*) with one of the neighbors. It was clear that everyone knows who Sara is and that they find comfort in her confidence, just like I do. "Aquí siempre se saluda, Laura" (*We always greet each other here, Laura*), she said, prompting me to also look up from my phone, look around, and smile as we approached the locally owned Mexican restaurant where we would have lunch.

I can't believe that I've lived in Michigan for over a year without making my way to the *tortas* in Grand Rapids before today. Immediately, life-altering goodness ensued in both food and conversation.

SARA: ¿Entonces, como te va Laura? Como te está gustando el trabajo?
(*So, how's it going, Laura. How are you liking the job?*)
LAURA: La verdad es que me encanta, pero a veces sí es un poco . . .
overwhelming. (*To be honest, I love it, but it's definitely a little . . .
overwhelming sometimes*)
SARA: Si, a veces es muy estresante. Pero vale la pena. (*Yes, sometimes
it's really stressful. But it's worth it*)

As we continued eating and laughing, I came to learn more about Sara's role in her community, and I acknowledged the powerful role that she has already come to play in my life even after just a few short weeks. Sara is a fighter like I've never seen before, experiencing all of life's challenges as an immigrant single mother who came to the US seeking happiness and stability, before learning quickly that this stability is granted to some and made impossible for others.

SARA: ¿Y, como te va con las traducciones? (*So, how's it going with the
translations?*).
LAURA: I like them. I mean, it's very hard for me because I was in third
grade when I stopped writing in Spanish at school. So, *me gusta
hablar más el Español que escribirlo, pero lo estoy aprendiendo nue-
vamente.* (*Me gustan. O sea, es muy difícil para mí porque yo solo es-
cribí el español en la escuela hasta el tercer grado. Entonces, I like
speaking Spanish more than I like writing it, but I'm learning it all
over again.*)
SARA: Yes, it's difficult to switch languages, but you will keep getting
better. The challenge is learning to adapt, *porque los lenguajes están
vivos* [because languages are alive], Laura—Language moves, it
breathes, it changes, and as translators we have to adapt with it.
That's a lot of work, and we have to do it every single day in every
single moment. We are the people who move this city. I'm so happy
you're here, amiga.
Yes, *amigas* (*friends*) indeed.

•   The journal excerpts shared here are only a glimpse into the many profound things that Sara understands and enacts about the power of language in her community. Through our work together, Sara taught me the connections between space, identity, language, and culture in a way that I had never before experienced. Always aware of her surroundings and her place in the community, Sara works as a force for those around her through every interaction—whether she is sitting in an office completing a written translation, driving around the city to facilitate verbal interpretation, or using her lunch break as an opportunity to greet and support local business owners in her city.

Sara's comment about the fluidity of language resonates with much of what I learned about language from sociolinguistics (García and Li Wei), which is unsurprising given Sara's training in neuropsychology and translation. Before coming into this office, I understood how language practices change based on cultural and rhetorical contexts. Yet, what became clear to me both through Sara's comment and through my ongoing work with the Language Services Department is that language does not only move and change—it also causes movement in its surrounding context; as Ríos puts it, "Space produces time rather than vice versa" ("Cultivating," 68). The movement that I traced in the Language Services Department did not just happen as words were transformed across Spanish and English. Instead, those linguistic transformations fueled material action, allowing children to enroll in school, community members to receive health services, and people to get the jobs they need to support their families in a different country.

Indeed, I later learned that the entire Hispanic Center of Western Michigan was first only a translation and interpretation office, one of the first Latinx community service centers to be established as part of larger efforts to mobilize and support Chicanx and Latinx communities in the Midwest. Thus, what I witnessed and participated in through my work with this organization was A Revised Rhetoric of Translation in action, through a small glimpse of a broader network established and sustained by Latinx communities in the United States who are seeking to get ahead despite all the adversity placed in front of them. From the beginning, the people in this organization have understood that the power of language extends beyond words. Translating documents and conversations is important, but it is only one piece of a bigger imperative in community action. Thus, analyzing the linguistic moves in this organization is only one piece of the puzzle, as it is also important to note how this linguistic activity impacts the broader movements within the city. From this understanding, I now turn to provide specific examples of the translation activities facilitated by the Language Services Department, illustrating how multilingual/ multimodal practices fuel the sustainability of an entire community.

"The People Who Move This City": Multimodal Translation Activities in the Language Services Department

Because the Language Services Department is founded on Sara's three-tiered model of community engagement, the goals and aims of the organization span beyond providing translation and interpretation services. The three-tiered approach and related organizational objectives inherently affect the daily activities of employees within this organization. For instance, translators act not only as adapters of language but also as community advocates, consulting with service providers to tailor information for Latinx communities rather than merely translating provided content. In addition, not only do employees translating legal documents aim to complete translation projects quickly to turn a profit, but they also seek to help community members use this translated information to fulfill material objectives like earning residency and employment. As Sara explained during an interview, activities within the Language Services Department are "always new, as you never know what you're going to get."

Understanding how employees navigate translation moments in the Language Services Department requires added attention to context and circumstance, following the first pillar of A Revised Rhetoric of Translation. Through this perspective, it is not enough simply to account for the objects facilitating translation and interpretation (e.g., computers, telephones, and translation tools and applications); it is also critical to account for the things being internalized and experienced both by the translators and by the community members throughout the translation process. A video montage is available (https://doi.org/10.3998/mpub.9952377. cmp.1) that provides a brief but contextualized illustration of the multilingual/multimodal activities and the movement that happens in the Language Services Department. This video introduces Sara as the director of the Language Services Department; Eloy, the coordinator who assigns interpretation jobs to other interpreters at the center; Carla, who is currently working as an interpreter; Graciela, a more experienced interpreter who has been working in the Language Services Department for over six years; and me, depicted as I interpret a phone call between a health service provider and a Spanish-speaking community member.

The video montage illustrates the constant movement and convergence of modalities—physical, material, and embodied (nonvisual)—that are enacted as professional translators and interpreters navigate translation moments. For instance, the video depicts Graciela explaining how interpreters have to work with health care providers and other clients to develop an adequate translation for Spanish-speaking community members. When Graciela says, "We were, like, writing, coloring, trying to get the point across, and we managed, but it was very difficult," she signals the ways in which interpreters have to combine visual and verbal modes to accomplish accurate translations. Furthermore, the examples shared by Graciela describe the immediacy and urgency through which successful interpretation happens. When interpreters are on a job, they translate information in the moment, with little time to second-guess their choices. Over time, interpreters develop a critical awareness of the kairotic impacts of translation, understanding, first, how the immediacy and urgency of any given situation may influence how information may be perceived by a particular individual and, second, how the information should be interpreted within the context of that situation. In these instances, interpreters like Graciela draw on a wide range of modalities and media to communicate information across languages.

In the video montage, Carla describes a translation moment that she experienced as she tried to translate the word *labor* in English for a mother who was giving birth. During this translation session, Carla explains, the doctor stated that he was going to "break [the patient's] water in order to get the labor started." In that moment, Carla had to make a decision about using the literal translation of the word *labor* in Spanish, which happens to be the same word. This literal translation for *labor* was referenced in one of Carla's training manuals on medical terminology, which directed her to translate *labor* in English with the same word in Spanish.

Rather than using the word *labor* in her translation, however, Carla decided to adjust the language and tell the Spanish-speaking client, "Le voy a romper la fuente para empezar con el nacimiento," which translates, "I'm going to break your water so that we can get the *birth* started." As Carla clarified in her conversation with the interpretation coordinator, Eloy, "I could have said 'to get the labor started,' but I knew in that moment that the patient could have misinterpreted the word *labor* to reference a job or profession." In this translation moment, Carla knew that she had to erase any potential confusion for the Spanish-speaking patient, especially during the intensity that is already overwhelming the mother giving birth. During this brief but critically important translation moment, Carla used her own experiences and her knowledge of Spanish and English to make a rhetorical decision that she then verbalized to the patient. Thus, Carla used multimodal strategies by rhetorically negotiating semiotic resources to reach a specific audience in a specific rhetorical situation.

In a follow-up artifact-based interview with me, Carla explained that in the specific translation moment discussed with Eloy, she "knew how scared" the patient giving birth was during this session. Because Carla is a mother herself, she understands the fear and stress that takes place during a birth. Recalling her experiences giving birth, Carla empathized with the patient during this high-stakes situation and decided to change the word she used, not because the use of *labor* is inaccurate but because Carla believed *nacimiento* (birth) would be a more effective and soothing word for the birthing mom to hear in this translation moment. As evidenced through this translation moment, when Carla interprets for her community, she draws both on her medical interpretation training and on her lived experiences as a Spanish-speaking Mexican American mother who struggled for years to navigate linguistic and cultural barriers on her own. Carla makes connections with the patients for whom she interprets, making important rhetorical decisions that take account both of "accurate" definitions of medical terminology and of contextual factors influencing the understanding of medical information in high-stakes environments. These decisions and the exigence that fuels them also render multimodal translation practices as translators work in digital environments to complete linguistic transformations for their community.

Digitally Mediated Multimodality in the Language Services Department

While interpreters like Carla and Graciela illustrate multimodal translation processes through their nonalphabetic, embodied experiences, other elements of multimodality also emerged as employees in the Language Services Department interacted with digital technologies in their written translations. For example, in a translation session shown briefly in the video montage mentioned above, Sara was translating a flyer regarding an event sponsored by the organization Heart of West Michigan United Way. As she read the English version of the flyer aloud during her translation process, Sara began gesturing back and forth with her fingers, pointing to the computer screen and moving her hands as she continued reading aloud. As she continued gesturing back and forth with her fingers, Sara said,

> I'm going to start later in the sentence, even though the English version starts with the words "Heart of West Michigan United Way." Rather than keeping

the order the same in Spanish, I'm going to start the translation in a different spot in the sentence, because if I start the translation with "Heart of West Michigan United Way," the Spanish-speaking reader will not be compelled to keep reading. Last time we did a flyer translation, when we started with the name of an organization in English, the Spanish-speaking clients did not feel like the flyer was intended for them. So here, I'm going to start differently.

During this translation moment, Sara combined the strategies of gesturing and reading aloud when making a decision about where to begin the Spanish version of this flyer. Sara was not necessarily struggling to come up with the translation of a specific word in Spanish. For this reason, using a digital translation tool would not have been useful in this instance. Instead, Sara used her own previous experiences ("Last time we did a flyer translation . . ."), as well as her own embodied practice during the invention process, to make a rhetorical decision that helped her overcome this translation moment. As Sara moved her fingers back and forth in front of the screen, she envisioned and decided between various sentence structures that would facilitate understanding for Spanish-speaking users interacting with this flyer. By moving her fingers across the screen, Sara visualized how the various grammatical structures could be presented in both Spanish and English, deciding to start her translation with a word in Spanish rather than keeping the English name of the organization at the beginning of the sentence. In this way, Sara used embodied strategies, through her gesturing at the screen, to navigate this particular translation moment.

As she continued translating this same flyer, Sara paused to decide how she would translate the word *champion* into Spanish. During this translation moment, Sara used the digital translation tool WordReference (http://www.wordreference.com/) to look for a word in Spanish that would signal a "champion" in health insurance rather than a champion of a race or sports event. As she considered WordReference's options to decide which word to use in her translation, Sara repeated each word provided by WordReference aloud, using her indexed cultural knowledge and lived experiences to decide which word most accurately matched the rhetorical situations in which she has used this term before. During this translation moment, Sara repeated the words *campeón* and *triunfador* (potential translations for English *champion*) over and over again during her translation process, attempting to trigger her memories regarding previous contexts in which she has seen these words. As she moved back and forth between these two options, Sara moved her fingers in front of the computer screen, pointing back and forth at each printed word on the screen and signaling a recursive back-and-forth movement as she made her final decision. As she moved through this translation, Sara continued to layer rhetorical strategies and modalities to transform information, using her body, her memory, and several digital tools to assist during this cyclical and recursive process, consequently echoing the second pillar of A Revised Rhetoric of Translation.

In another project (not included in the introductory video montage), Catalina, another translator for the Language Services Department, was working to translate a marriage certificate for a community client. During this process, Catalina experienced a translation moment as she paused to decide how to translate the word *notarize* in reference to the marriage certificate being legally issued and notarized in a government agency. At first, Catalina used the Linguee digital translator to look up Spanish translations for the word *notarize*. Linguee provided three possible Spanish words: *notariado*, *notarizado*, and *escriturado*. While these translations were helpful, all three translation options were provided by Linguee as present-tense adjectives, and Catalina was looking for a past-tense description. During this translation moment, Catalina was left to improvise a translation.

At first, Catalina asked out loud as she was translating in the office of the Language Services Department, "Como dirían 'notarized'?" (*How would you all say "notarized"?*). Sara, who happened to be in the office at the time, responded to Catalina by stating, "*Notarizado?*" Catalina replied, "Yeah, I think so, *pero* [but] what about *notariado*?" Catalina and Sara then repeated both words interchangeably aloud several times, "*Notariado, notarizado, notariado, notarizado*—which sounds better?" They then Googled both words to find examples of each used in articles written in Spanish. At this point, Sara explained, "I think *notariado* is the correct translation grammatically speaking, but *notarizado* is used most commonly in practice." Based on this conversation and on their collaborative research, Catalina used *notarizado* in her translation.

Like Sara's repetition of the Spanish translation options for the word *champion* (*campeón* and *triunfador*), Catalina and Sara's repetition of the words *notariado* and *notarizado* served as memory triggers that, in combination with the digital platforms of Linguee and word-processing software, assisted in navigating translation moments both accurately and successfully. Neither Catalina nor Sara could find a definite answer online to navigate this translation, but through their combined experiences and their collaborative effort to figure out what "sounds right" by repeating translation options out loud, Catalina and Sara reached an effective translation in this translation moment.

In these brief examples, the combination of digital and material modes led the professional translators and interpreters Sara, Catalina, and Carla to reach effective translations that adequately reflected the digital and cultural needs and values of their respective Spanish-speaking audiences. While translators in this professional office used deconstructing, gesturing, repeating, and storytelling strategies like those use by the translators at KLN (discussed in chapter 5), the added lived experiences and training of translators like Catalina, Carla, and Sara allowed them to make more connections between what is considered an "accurate" translation by a dictionary or digital tool and what may be understood most successfully by Spanish-speaking clients experiencing urgent and important situations. These connections to previous experiences and the coordination of technological and cultural resources continued to gain importance as translators worked to complete visual multimodal projects.

Mirror Translations in the Language Services Department: Visual Multimodality across Languages

In addition to digital platforms like Linguee, WordReference, and Google Translate, employees in the Language Services Department enacted multimodal translation practices through their visual translation projects. While the Language Services Department facilitates many different types of written and verbal translation projects (e.g., medical interpretation sessions on the phone and in person, website translations, and flyer translations), the most common type of project to enter the Language Services Department is the translation of technical documents such as birth certificates, legal documents (e.g., court reports), and education records. After moving to the United States from other North American, South American, and Central American countries, Latinx community members often have to translate technical documents in order to establish official residency, enroll in school, and qualify for health insurance (among other purposes). For this reason, the Language Services Department provides low-cost document translation to community members. During my work with the Language Services Department in 2015, employees in this office translated approximately fifty-six hundred legal, medical, and education documents for members of the community.

Although the language on these types of technical documents is often limited (ranging from one to two pages and from one hundred to three hundred words), much of the work in these types of translations requires that translators design and redesign logos, seals, and other visuals across languages. To ease language accessibility in technical translations and to ensure that government agencies will accept translated technical documents, the Language Services Department provides clients with "mirror translations," which consist of translated documents that identically match the design, layout, and formatting of the original text (Pym, 486). Because the Language Services Department provides mirror translations, graphics like the seals must be translated and designed before the translated document is considered complete. Due to the frequency of translations requiring seals (birth certificates, proof of something, etc.), the Language Services Department's greatest source of intellectual property has become their extensive, editable, document library of translated seals. Translators have built this extensive database of translated seals and stamps over the course of twenty-seven years. Seals and stamps are organized into the categories of birth/death/marriage certificates, educational/medical records, and other document templates, organized by the country of origin of each original text. Figures 10–12 illustrate various seals and figures that were designed by translators during the period of my data collection in the Language Services Department.

The image at the top of figure 10 is a picture from an original Mexican birth certificate seal submitted for translation at the Language Services Department. The image on the bottom is a screenshot from the translated seal designed by a translator in the department. As evidenced in these two images, employees in the Language Services Department must both translate the information contained in the seal (e.g., "Office of the Civil Registry") and include the images and logos in the translated document, for reference. In this way, translators act also as designers in the translation of birth certificates, ensuring the usability of translated documents by providing mirror translations that can be clearly understood in both the original language and the target language.

The image at the top of figure 11 is a picture from an original Cuban education certificate submitted by a client of the Language Services Department. On the bottom is the image designed and translated by an employee from the department. The translated phrase "sealed species," which signals that the client paid the taxes due on her original document, provides added credibility to the translated document, indicating to an English-speaking reader that the educational record was submitted to and accepted by the Cuban embassy.

In recent years, government agencies have been providing ways for individuals to digitally verify the authenticity of technical documents such as birth certificates. Although translators cannot re-create digital barcodes on

365085–365085

Fig. 10. Original (*top*) and translation (*bottom*) of a birth certificate seal from Tepehuanes, Durango, Mexico

Fig. 11. Original (*top*) and translation (*bottom*) of an educational record stamp from Cuba

Fig. 12. Birth certificate seals and seal barcodes from the Dominican Republic, original (*top*) and translation (*bottom*)

birth certificates and other documents (as depicted in fig. 12), it is important for translators to place barcodes and their corresponding verification numbers in the right position on finalized documents. In this way, government agencies can verify the validity of these technical documents via a verification number.

As evidenced in figures 10–12, the translation of technical documents, at least for participants in the Language Services Department, inherently requires multilingual, multimodal design that stems beyond alphabetic writing in a single language. Indeed, in the video and screencast footage that I recorded during my time working and researching in the Language Services Department, 65 percent of the time translators spent in the translation of technical documents was focused on designing logos and images, to render translations that make sense visually and alphabetically in both English and Spanish for specific purposes and contexts. During an interview, one translator, Holly, explained that her time spent translating a single birth certificate encompassed "thirty minutes total: ten minutes translating the text, twenty minutes fixing seal graphic templates." Since the Language Services Department has been in business for twenty-seven years and since all translations completed at the Hispanic Center are stored on a secure server, previous translations are used as templates for new projects, decreasing the amount of time that translators have to spend recreating frequently used seals and images. For instance, Mexican state seals that have remained the same for decades are copied into new technical document translations repeatedly. However, as Holly explained in her description of "fixing seal graphic templates," although the Language Services Department has this extensive library of translated seals, their insertion into documents still requires formatting and manipulation to completely mirror and communicate (to the best of the translator's ability) the original document. In the case of technical translations such as birth and marriage certificates, multimodality is enacted both through the combination of images and words on final translated documents and through the embodied, material modes deployed by translators like Sara and Catalina as they consult each other and their own lived experiences when making decisions in the moment of translation.

In addition to mirror translations of technical documents, translators in the Language Services Department often have to navigate other visual digitally designed elements in their translation projects. During my work in the Language Services Department office, a local institution that was preparing information materials regarding home foreclosure issues for community members in Michigan requested the translation of a seven-part document (127 total pages). The institution sought to have these documents available in English and Spanish on their website, so that members of the Latinx community could utilize the institution's services. In particular, the institution aimed to provide resources (in both Spanish and English) to help community members understand and navigate through processes of home foreclosure. This translation project consisted of translating an entire website, with hyperlinks to external content.

When the Language Services Department originally received this translation request, I observed a conversation between Sara and Holly, where they discussed the value of this project. "This is a great resource for our people," said Sara, adding, "They can really use information on foreclosure." Holly then replied, "Yes, but *how* are we going to do it?" To complete this translation request, translators not only had to complete mirror translations, which included formatting and designing to match the original website. They also had to delegate discrete translation and design activities to different team members, as well as design the translations with the end users, client, and web developers in mind. Thus, the translators engaged in multiple, overlapping multimodal activities normally undertaken by specialized project managers, translators, user experience designers, and web developers. Since the Language Services Department is a small, low-budget office and since translators for the organization are trained bilingual community members who typically have not had extensive professional technological training outside of the office, technical equipment (e.g., design software) is not readily available. Instead, translators have to work with limited software (e.g., Microsoft Office) to complete all projects.

In addition to translating technical language about home financing and foreclosure, the four translators who worked on this project had to negotiate roles as project managers and designers. The 127-page file was initially delivered to the office as a PDF document (see fig. 13). Later, after a client conversation regarding formatting and style, the document was resubmitted by the client as an editable Microsoft Word file. Translators worked on this editable Word file to complete and format the initial translation, taking into account visuals that could be seen directly on the document in which they were working. However, three weeks into the project (after all the language translation had been completed), the client contacted the Language Services Department to request that the content be reformatted into a file format that would make the content suitable for transfer into web publishing (see fig. 14). This last-minute reformatting, which facilitated web design and online accessibility, resulted in an additional fifty hours of work for the Language Services Department, because the formatting update requested by the client required knowledge in web coding (marking spaces, headings, etc.) that was not readily available to participants in the department. In turn, to complete this reformatting, translators had to learn to navigate new software (SDL Trados, a popular digital translation tool), while simultaneously keeping in mind how this new translation format might impact Spanish-speaking readers aiming to understand the content in the finished project. Reformatting this document required translators to understand how English content was segmented in the original version and then to develop a way to similarly break up Spanish content in a way that would fit within the specified parameters of the new format.

As figure 13 illustrates, the content presented in the original document allowed translators to see how information would be presented to the target audiences. Translators working in this document could see the images and space limitations and could make translation choices based on these parameters. In the reformatted version depicted in figure 14, however, information is broken into line segments. Translators working with this document do not always have a reference point for how their words will be

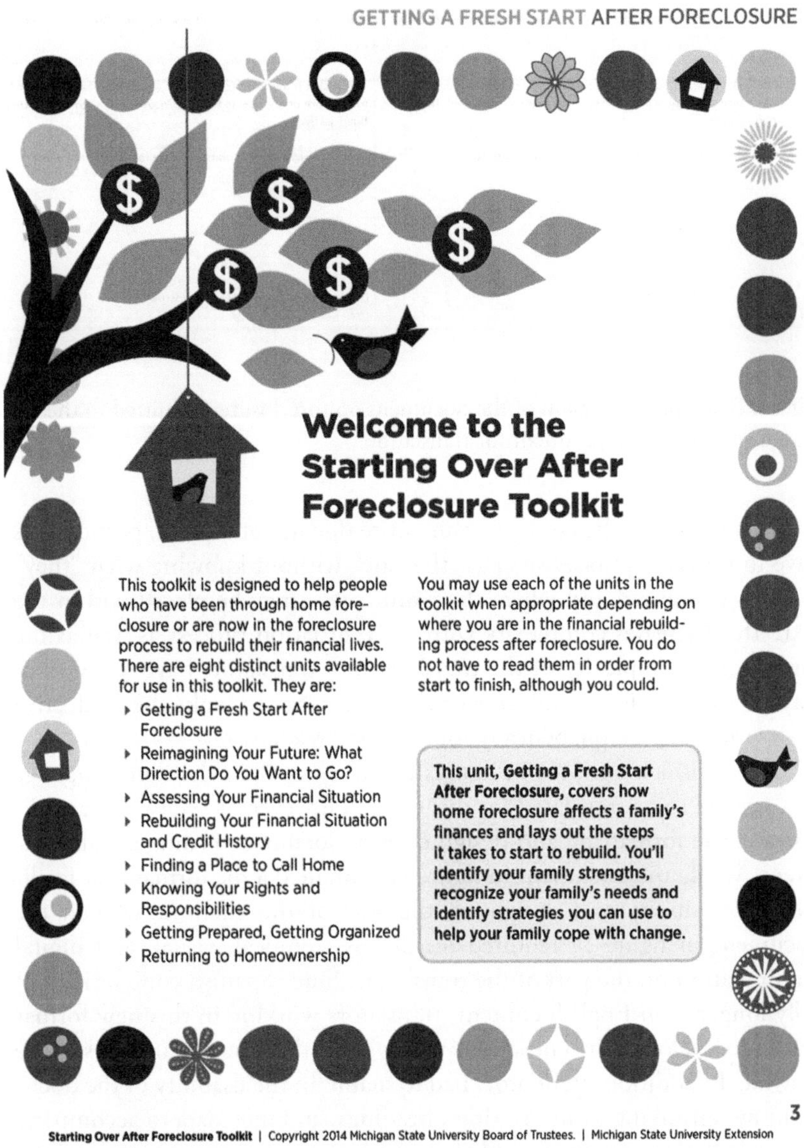

Welcome to the Starting Over After Foreclosure Toolkit

This toolkit is designed to help people who have been through home foreclosure or are now in the foreclosure process to rebuild their financial lives. There are eight distinct units available for use in this toolkit. They are:

▸ Getting a Fresh Start After Foreclosure
▸ Reimagining Your Future: What Direction Do You Want to Go?
▸ Assessing Your Financial Situation
▸ Rebuilding Your Financial Situation and Credit History
▸ Finding a Place to Call Home
▸ Knowing Your Rights and Responsibilities
▸ Getting Prepared, Getting Organized
▸ Returning to Homeownership

You may use each of the units in the toolkit when appropriate depending on where you are in the financial rebuilding process after foreclosure. You do not have to read them in order from start to finish, although you could.

This unit, **Getting a Fresh Start After Foreclosure**, covers how home foreclosure affects a family's finances and lays out the steps it takes to start to rebuild. You'll identify your family strengths, recognize your family's needs and identify strategies you can use to help your family cope with change.

3

Fig. 13. Initial PDF document on foreclosure submitted to the Language Services Department for translation

48	Not Transl ated (0%)	<181/><182/>Welcome to the Starting Over After Foreclosure Toolkit	<181/><182/>Welcome to the Starting Over After Foreclosure Toolkit
49	Not Transl ated (0%)	This toolkit is designed to help people who have been through home foreclosure or are now in the foreclosure process to rebuild their financial lives.	This toolkit is designed to help people who have been through home foreclosure or are now in the foreclosure process to rebuild their financial lives.
50	Not Transl ated (0%)	There are eight distinct units available for use in this toolkit.	There are eight distinct units available for use in this toolkit.
51	Not Transl ated (0%)	They are:	They are:
52	Not Transl ated (0%)	Getting a Fresh Start After Foreclosure	Getting a Fresh Start After Foreclosure

Fig. 14. Reformatted version of the document on foreclosure submitted to the Language Services Department for translation

positioned within the context of an entire document; that is, participants have to translate phrases such as "they are" without knowing what "they" is being referenced and where the word "they" may be placed within the text. This increases complexity with the translation process as well as the multimodal complexity of the translation, as translators have to think of ways to rhetorically reposition words in a sentence to make them effective both visually and alphabetically for intended readers.

The documents shown in figures 13 and 14 contain the same language that needed to be translated for this client. However, as the two images illustrate, the formatting and design of each document is dramatically different. While the document in figure 13 contained a file format that facilitated accessibility and design on the side of the client developer, the document in figure 14 required much less technical, visual, and digital manipulation on the part of the translators. Since Spanish content is typically longer than English content, translators working in this new format had to redevelop their translations to fit within the space boundaries of the new file. In addition, translators had to maintain the usability of the document by rethinking captions, titles, headings, and metadata to accompany their translations in this new file format.

During an interview, Sara (who worked as one of the translators on the foreclosure project) explained that the updated file format was "challenging" for their office.

We had to think of new ways to translate information, even though we had already technically completed the translation in the first file version. The purpose of this new format was to publish something on the web, which was not clear to us in the original version. This completely changes the translation because now we have to think about words *and* space, numbers [with the line segments] *and* letters, as well as visuals, all while keeping our community in mind and thinking about how they would be using their information. We can't send them to a hyperlink that is not translated or break up a title just because there is a picture in between the words. We have to think of ways to redirect the information so that it's available and understandable to them in their language. It's not just about replacing words." (emphasis added)

Sara's reference to the overlapping activities completed by translators within the Language Services Department (in her discussion of "words and space, numbers and letters") reflects the constant flux of activity that participants in this organization must undertake to successfully complete such a large-scale translation project. Through my observation and participation in this specific translation, I was able to note the various dimensions of multimodality being enacted by translators as they considered how to rhetorically reposition content for their communities. For instance, because the translators in the Language Services Department are experts when it comes to understanding how speakers of Spanish read in Spanish, they can understand how readers of Spanish might navigate information differently than those who can read the information in English. The line segments and text breaks embedded in the reformatted file were created with speakers and readers of English in mind, which meant that the translators were left to make decisions about how these formats could impact their audience. Although translators in the Language Services Department are not formally trained in user experience or web development, these individuals are, as Sara demonstrates, the ones with expertise in these instances, leveraging their cultural and linguistic knowledge across modes, platforms, and media in order to successfully complete their work. Only through interactions among these composing elements are translation projects both effectively completed and holistically understood.

Multimodal Elements Coming Together

This chapter provides several examples of how multilingual and multimodal elements of translation come together in the work of professional translators and interpreters. Mirror translations, web content analysis, and cultural representations are all incorporated into the daily realities of employees in the Language Services Department. In addition, translators in that office represent a wide range of generational and socioeconomic distributions. They have extensive lived experiences to draw from when completing their work, and they serve multiple different parts of their community, working across medical, legal, and educational contexts rather than being constrained to translating in one area.

What most struck me about the translation work completed in the Language Services Department is the immediate impact that professional translation and interpretation activities have on the community members in the surrounding area. While I can separate and analyze the individual multimodal elements enacted through translation in material and digital environments in the Language Services Department, there were certain moments in my experiences with this organization that pushed all of these resources and practices to come together. While analyzing the individual translation moments in this organization helped me see the interactions between the different modes and languages used by translators, witnessing the force behind these individual elements in the lives of human beings helped me further understand how linguistic, technological, and material resources must be combined to render successful community action. To help close this chapter, I share a story that further illustrates the depth, exigence, and power that results when all the multilingual/multimodal elements of translation come together.

Teresa's Story

During one of my last weeks working in the office of the Language Services Department, I was fortunate to meet Teresa, a community client who came into the office requesting help with a written translation. I vividly remember getting up to greet Teresa after she walked in and requested the translation of a 125-page document that she clenched tightly between her fingers. Figure 15 shows the first page of Teresa's document, both in the original Spanish and in the translated English version. The complete document contained over 37,000 words and included several hundred seals, logos, and images.

Upon first assessing Teresa's document, I immediately realized that, even at the discounted pricing that the department offered to community members, this translation would cost Teresa over two thousand dollars to complete, particularly because the project would require both translating the alphabetic words and recreating the images included in the text. As I initially discussed this translation project with Teresa

Fig. 15. Original (*left*) and translation (*right*) of the first page in a document submitted to the Language Services Department by the client Teresa

throughout our consultation, I thought about the different layers of complexity embedded in the document. As a technical translator, I analyzed the linguistic complexity of the text, reading through the legal language and immediately attempting to determine which of the translators would be most suited for this project. I also asked some questions about the translation, trying to find ways to reduce the cost of the project: "Gracias por venir, señora Teresa. Parece que este proyecto es muy importante, pero también está muy complicado. ¿Sera que tiene que traducir todas las hojas, o podríamos omitir algunas para reducir el costo?" (*Thanks for coming in, Ms. Teresa. It looks like this project is really important, but it's also really complicated. Are you sure that you have to have all the pages translated, or can we omit some pages to reduce the cost?*) As a human reading through this document in Teresa's presence, I couldn't help but notice Teresa's eyes water, her eyebrows scrunch, and her hands tense up into fists, trying to find strength as I flipped through the pages that contained her story (rather than just my project): "No, sí tengo que traducir todas las hojas. Es lo único que tengo. Tengo que traducirlo todo completo." (*No, I do have to have all the pages translated. It's the only thing I have. I have to translate everything completely.*)

Through our conversation and upon further analysis of the document, I found out that it was the only documentation Teresa was given following her husband's work-related fatal accident in Mexico. Teresa's husband had left Grand Rapids to complete a construction project in Mexico, expecting to return within a month of his departure. Weeks after her husband was scheduled to return to their home in Grand Rapids, however, Teresa received this 125-page document in the mail, with no other explanation of what had happened. She broke into tears as she recalled, "Ni una llamada, ni una explicación; solo me enviaron este documento por correo" (*Not even a phone call, not one explanation; they just mailed me this document*). Teresa proceeded to explain that she needed to contract a lawyer in the United States to pursue legal compensation for the tragedy described in her document. Although she had found and was currently working with a successful lawyer, Teresa soon found out that the lawyer (who was not proficient in Spanish) needed the document to be translated and notarized before he could begin Teresa's case. For this reason, Teresa walked into the Language Services Department requesting assistance, holding this intricate document that contained all her hope for potential justice. She explained, "Tengo que contratar a este abogado y tengo que buscar justicia" (*I have to work with this lawyer, and I have to seek justice*).

Completing Teresa's translation required conversations among translators, Teresa, her lawyer, and other legal experts. In addition, completing mirror translations of the seal and logo included in Teresa's document required the rhetorical manipulation of visuals, completed over several weeks through the use of in-house digital tools like Microsoft Word and PowerPoint, in combination with alphabetic translations completed with the assistance of cultural knowledge and digital tools like Linguee and Google Translate. In short, successfully completing translations in a professional office like the Language Services Department inherently required the "thoughtful and aware modification [of texts, visuals, and other modes] for particular audiences and circumstances," circumstances that sometimes, as Teresa's case illustrates, hold the highest stakes and most drastic potential consequences (Arola, Sheppard, and Ball, "Multimodality").

Although Teresa's case may seem extreme, every document translation—every birth, death, vaccination, education, marriage, and/or divorce certificate—contains a story that starts before the document comes into the office, continues as translators navigate the visual and alphabetic conversion of the text across languages, and evolves through the continued interactions that are facilitated through the document after it leaves the office. Translation projects like the ones completed in the Language Services Department embody multimodal elements both in practice and product, taking shape in and through the human and technological interactions that fuel their development. In Teresa's particular case, understanding the story behind the 125-page document helped employees in the Language Services Department find external funding to facilitate the translation. Through our work with Teresa and other translators in the Language Services Department, we were able both to find funds for this project and to understand the care that needed to be taken with this translation if it was to positively influence the lawyer's case on behalf of Teresa and her late husband. If we had only acknowledged this as a standard translation project, we may have missed the depth of this work and the injustice that led to its development in the first place, not understanding the urgency of the project and the impact of the consequences relying on its completion. Personal interactions with Teresa gave us the opportunity to complete the translation in an ethical and effective manner.

While there are typically several technical and intellectual practices at play in the completion of professional translation, the biggest motivator for this work is the continued livelihood of the people relying on the information being transformed across languages. The focus and exigency for thoroughly understanding professional translation, then, is less the individual words, phrases, and visuals being transformed than the lives that are transformed in conjunction. Multilingual/multimodal activities embedded in these translations are the catalysts for community action, continuously influencing and being influenced by the lives, experiences, and needs of the individuals who make this work possible.

• Understanding the stories behind translation, especially in a community organization such as the Language Services Department, requires intricate attention to both process and practice in multilingual, multimodal communication. As Sara mentioned to me during our early interactions, you cannot truly understand translation without actually being a part of the work itself—understanding the various exigencies that drive its completion. To be sure, not all translation work is as intense as the work that is completed in the Language Services Department. Translation work in business settings, for instance, may be completed for entirely different reasons than the translations I witnessed in my small community organization. Yet, although the work of translation may be abstracted and discussed in technical terms alone, understanding the experiences of the translators themselves and getting a sense of the rhetorical activities embedded in language transformation allows us to better account for the labor that often remains invisible when we discuss multimodal and multilingual communication in both academic and professional settings.

As scholars and teachers in rhetoric and composition, technical communication, and related areas continue to make connections between multilingualism and multimodality, I encourage us to think both about multilingual/multimodal texts and projects and about the practices and stories that lead to these productions. Although the multimodal activities and practices encompassed in translation projects within both KLN (discussed in chapter 5) and the Language Services Department took place mostly outside of traditional classrooms, rhetoric and composition scholarship has taught us enough to understand that our students' experiences extend through and beyond the constraints of our classroom spaces and assignments. For this reason, as Shipka urges, it is important for writing researchers and teachers to understand and value the "roles [that] texts, talk, people, perceptions, semiotic resources, technologies, motives, activities, and institutions play in the production, reception, circulation, and valuation of seemingly stable finished texts" (*Toward a Composition*, 13). At both KLN and in the Language Services Department, no form of communication was fixed or stable; in fact, it was this instability and constant flux that made translators like Brigitte, Natalie, and Sara so powerful and capable as multilingual/multimodal rhetoricians and technical communicators. In chapter 7, as I present implications for these case studies, I further illustrate how A Revised Rhetoric of Translation, as it was developed through the work of translations at KLN and in the Language Services Department, can help us continue to situate multilingual/multimodal communication in the lived experiences of students and professionals from a wide range of backgrounds.

7 • Using Translation Frameworks to Research, Teach, and Practice Multilingual/ Multimodal Communication

As I was wrapping up my work with both KLN and the Language Services Department, I also entered the academic job market, applying and interviewing for faculty positions with specializations in both rhetoric and composition and technical communication. While interviewing at different stages and sharing this project with people at institutions in various parts of the United States, I frequently got asked different versions of the same question: "Your work on translation and multilingual/multimodal communication is interesting, but (how) is it relevant *here?*" (Gonzales, "But Is That Relevant *Here?*"). While continued growth in international student enrollment in U.S. colleges and universities has led to increased need for training in multilingual communication (Redden), these conversations clarified for me that issues of language diversity are still sometimes segmented and positioned as only relevant to departments and institutions with large numbers of nontraditional students. In predominantly white institutions and in departments with small numbers of students who identify as multilingual, research on and practices about multilingual communication (e.g., the translation work presented through the project discussed in this book) are sometimes deemed interesting at best and irrelevant more broadly. In rhetoric and composition specifically, students who are institutionally classified as "English language learners," "L2 learners," or "multilingual learners/writers" or who are given other institutional labels to signal linguistic difference are sometimes assigned to remedial, basic, or pre-composition courses. This common practice can deem "traditional" writing courses, students, and faculty as presumably free from the responsibility of acknowledging and addressing language difference and its presence in all contemporary classrooms (Matsuda).

I aim to articulate more directly in this chapter that research on translation and multilingual communication, such as the case studies in chapters 5 and 6, is relevant and valuable to all facets of writing research, instruction, and practice. Rather than positioning translation as something relevant only to students and communicators who transform information across named languages (e.g., English and Spanish), I argue that writing researchers and teachers should recognize translation as a foundational activity for all writers and communicators, particularly if our disciplines and fields want to continue expanding our notions of writing beyond standard alphabetic modalities. Rather than segmenting translation work to something that only multilingual communicators do, we might recognize translation work of multilinguals as a model of how ideas can be rhetorically transformed for various audiences, learning from the multimodal strategies that multilingual communicators use to adapt their ideas across contexts and communities. It is key that we not only recognize that translation as relevant to all communication but also use translation frameworks to intricately account for ranges and dimensions of communicative fluidity in culturally situated contexts, leveraging (rather than flattening) difference as an opportunity for rhetorical action. To this end, this chapter provides specific implications for how the translation framework presented in the project discussed in this book can inform writing research and pedagogies across fields and disciplines.

Using Translation Moments to Research and Teach Multimodality and Digital Rhetoric

Chapters 5 and 6 present examples of various translation processes enacted by both student translators in a university organization and professional translators in a small business that offers language services. It is important to note that the translation process of each participant in my research was unique and directly related to the participant's own history and lived experiences. Yet, by analyzing these diverse practices across contexts and zooming in on how translation practices are negotiated during translation moments, I was able to trace some patterns in the strategies frequently deployed by translators as they adapt information across languages. These patterns and strategies (introduced in chapter 2) are further illustrated in figure 16.

The translation strategies depicted in figure 16 (e.g., negotiating, repeating, gesturing) were deployed and layered by multilingual communicators during translation moments, when translators used a variety of se-

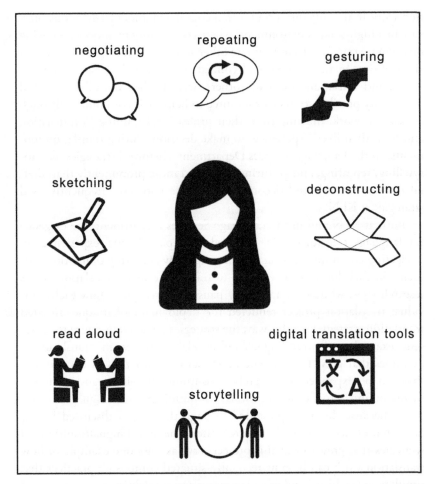

Fig. 16. Frequent strategies used in translation

miotic resources to transform a specific word or phrase for a specific audience in a particular rhetorical context. At KLN, translation strategies like negotiating and using digital translation tools were used by participants as they translated news stories from English to Spanish for their community. In this specific context, translators like Natalie and Brigitte used their cultural and technological expertise to manipulate the algorithms of digital translation tools in a way that helped them develop more options for conveying meaning to their audience in Orlando.

In the Language Services Department, the translation strategies depicted in figure 16 were used differently, particularly because the translation work in that organization is often completed under tremendous pressure in a high-stakes environment, where community members are relying on accurate translations to facilitate other activities that impact their material realities. In this professional context, translators like Sara, Catalina, Holly, and Carla, among many others, were pushed to collaborate and deploy any possible strategy or resource to help their community through translation work, drawing from their professional training in translation and from their lived experiences to make decisions during translation moments. In the Language Services Department, rhetorical strategies like storytelling, repeating, and gesturing were used more prominently than digital translation tools and deconstructing—the two most frequently used strategies at KLN.

Both at KLN and in the Language Services Department, the exigency for language transformation is paired with participants' experiences in navigating communication across languages. By analyzing translation moments in each location, I was able to trace patterns in translation across research sites, while simultaneously pausing to recognize how each individual translation project rendered the deployment of unique, situated translation strategies. In this way, the strategies depicted in figure 16 represent examples of multilingual/multimodal activities in translation— examples that grew from situated analyses of translation in context and that can be expanded as researchers continue studying translation moments in and across other locations, communities, and languages. In essence, because the work presented through the project discussed in this book represents two small research sites, the multilingual/multimodal strategies that grew out of this project serve as only one example of how translation work can help us recognize situated composing practices that simultaneously blend and cross languages and modalities.

Gunther Kress explains that the concept of "mode" (rooting the term *multimodality*) is "a term that allows us to get away from using language for everything. In other words, you might say there's visual language, and there's gestural language, and there is a language of flowers. We now say there are different modes, and modes are resources whereby we can make meaning material" ("What Is a Mode?"). In professional/technical translation work, a reliance on alphabetic language is often inefficient, as the whole challenge of the translation activity is to convey meaning beyond linguistic barriers by using whatever resources are most effective or readily available. Sometimes, linguistic translations come through easily, but often, as evidenced in the translation moments depicted in chapters 5 and 6, alphabetic language is not the most reliable source of communication, leading translators to leverage other modes to transform meaning. By using rhetorical strategies like gesturing, sketching, or seeking information using digital translation tools, translators enact multimodal communication, moving away from "using language for everything" to using the most effective mode to convey a specific word or idea for a specific audience.

By learning about the translation strategies of multilingual communicators, writers of all backgrounds can intricately see the connections between modalities and rhetoric, using and expanding the strategies presented in figure 16 to describe how communicators can layer and repurpose meaning across languages and modes simultaneously, for specific rhetorical purposes. Because the multimodal elements of translation are enacted based on rhetorical exigencies, understanding and teaching multimodality through translation work allows us to keep rhetorical purpose and modality use in conjunction. In using translation and translation moments as a framework to teach multimodality in rhetoric and composition, we can continue to illustrate how, as Arola, Ball, and Sheppard remind us, multimodality is always inherently tied to and motivated by rhetoric. Likewise, by understanding the technical elements embedded in translation (e.g., visuals, logos, and seals in mirror translations) and by linking these elements to the professional needs and experiences of multilinguals, technical and professional writers can also trace translation moments experienced in professional contexts as information is made accessible to linguistically diverse users.

In addition to analyzing the translation moments like the ones shared in this book, writers can document and analyze how they navigate translation moments to various degrees in their daily activities, whether they are translating across named languages, within the same language, and/or across various digital tools and platforms. By pausing to recognize when we experience translation moments and by tracing the semiotic resources and practices that we deploy to navigate these moments, we can continue to account for the ways in which our multimodal composing practices are always tied to broader discursive goals. Using translation moments as analytical units can help us see ranges and degrees in language fluidity and how we deploy specific communicative practices when communicating with different audiences. Rather than flattening language difference by merely saying that everyone translates, translation moments allow us to see how, when, and why translators use different rhetorical strategies to make information accessible for specific audiences at specific moments in time.

Using A Revised Rhetoric of Translation to Connect Languages, Modalities, and Cultures

While the concept of translation moments can be used to analyze the specific multilingual and multimodal elements deployed in language transformation, the framework of A Revised Rhetoric of Translation allows us to make deeper connections between these multilingual/multimodal translation elements and their surrounding cultural influences. As Kress ("What Is a Mode?") clarifies, modes are "*cultural* resources for making meaning," practices situated within our lived existences that allow us to make (and interpret) meaning through touch, visuals, smell, and more. Putting Kress's definition of modes in conversation with the lived experiences of multilinguals who navigate meaning across languages, we can see that the modalities that communicators choose to use and the modalities that specific communicators can interpret are entirely dependent on several cultural factors. For translators like Sara, Brigitte, Natalie, and others, working across semiotic resources and layering communicative practices is not a stylistic choice or preference. Instead, translation practices are situated both in a specific rhetorical situation (e.g., the transformation of a birth certificate from Spanish to English) and in the cultural history and experience of the individual translator(s) completing this task. For example, if Sara in the Language Services Department is translating a birth certificate, the strategies she uses to navigate translation moments in that project will depend both on the situation that prompted the exigency for the translation (e.g., a mother needs to enroll her child in school) and on Sara's skills, training, and experience (e.g., Sara's cultural background, her training and knowledge of translation dictionaries, and how she may be feeling on the day that the translation project arrived). Thus, orienting to translation work through A Revised Rhetoric of Translation can help researchers, teachers, and practitioners of writing to understand the cultural influences and the rhetorical context fueling linguistic choices in a specific moment.

In "Cultivating a Rhetorical Sensibility in the Translingual Writing Classroom," Juan Guerra illustrates the importance of connecting communicative practices to culture and experience.

> We falter in our efforts to help our students understand what a translingual approach is because we have been leading them to think that we expect them to produce a particular kind of writing that mimics what we call code-meshing rather than getting them to understand that what we want instead is for them

to call on the rhetorical sensibilities many of them already possess but put aside because of what they see as a jarring shift in context. (231–32)

As Guerra argues, the reason some recent efforts to embed linguistic difference in the composition classroom have been unsuccessful is not because writing teachers are failing to encourage students to use their entire linguistic and composing resources. Rather, these pedagogical challenges arise when teachers fail to understand how students' linguistic resources are always tied to broader cultural-rhetorical contexts. In other words, we experience challenges in teaching language diversity when we tell students to translanguage (to work across languages and modalities in the classroom) without setting up the cultural-rhetorical environment that will facilitate these interactions.

Rather than merely pushing students to incorporate modes and languages in our classroom projects, A Revised Rhetoric of Translation teaches us the importance of recognizing how these languages and modes are tied to various histories and lived experiences, as well as how the specific layering of these communicative resources and practices may have real consequences in the lives of our students and their communities. Just as Carla in the Language Services Department relived her experiences as a mother when interpreting for a patient during a birth, students in our classrooms and professionals in our workplaces may be both reliving and sharing their lived experiences as they blend languages and semiotic resources through their work. Translating and translanguaging thus requires teachers and researchers of rhetoric and writing to support the language work in which students and professionals engage and to appreciate the practices that students deploy, not as adherences to or deviations from our own expectations, but as evidence of multilinguals' own rhetorical and cultural labor.

Putting "context aside" is impossible within the framework of A Revised Rhetoric of Translation, as evidenced by the experiences of the translators depicted in this book. When clients like Teresa walk into the Language Services Department, they put a face and a story to the work of translation, causing translators like Sara and Catalina to develop the rhetorical sensibility needed (Lorimer Leonard) to understand the context and exigency for the multilingual, multimodal work in which they will engage to translate Teresa's documents. Similarly, student translators at KLN frequently reflect on their own educational and personal experiences as they translate for their community. They frequently reference "their" Latinx community in "their" city of Orlando, bringing with them a critical understanding of how their translation choices (and the semiotic resources that they incorporate into these choices) may be perceived by audiences from a specific physical location and from the various cultures represented in the same city. Thus, for the translators depicted in this book and, as Alanna Frost and Suzanne Blum Malley remind us, for multilinguals in general, "modality matters," and choosing the wrong language or mode in a specific interaction may render drastic consequences, both for the individual translating and for the audiences or clients receiving the translation work.

As writing researchers, teachers, and practitioners continue developing models for discussing language fluidity, I encourage us to keep in mind the cultural situatedness of language use, resisting the tendency to generalize or perhaps unintentionally erase layers and dimensions of cultural difference as we argue for all language as "multilingual" or "translingual." I hope that we can use the framework of A Revised Rhetoric of Translation to continue to recognize that all composing and communicative acts are different in very unique, cultural and rhetorical ways and require acts of translation (Gilyard). By continuing to listen for this communicative difference through frameworks like the one presented in this book, we can continue recognizing (rather than erasing) the dimensions, ranges, and intellectual work embedded in the multilingual/multimodal practices already being enacted in our classrooms, professions, and communities, with and without our prompting.

• By sharing stories of the translators who were gracious enough to be included in this book, I sought to make an intervention in contemporary conversations about language diversity in writing research and instruction, allowing us a space to pause within our discussions of language fluidity to further understand how language is transformed and repurposed by individuals who identify with heritage languages other than standardized Englishes. Through this discussion, I aimed both to illustrate how multilingual communicators navigate languages and technologies simultaneously and to reposition the work of translation as a cultural-rhetorical strategy, or techne, in itself.

In "Wampum as Hypertext," Angela Haas urges researchers to "resist the dominant notions of what it means to be technologically 'literate' or 'advanced,'" pushing us to "critically reflect on the struggles for and engage with discussions [about] digital and visual rhetorical sovereignty" (95). In linking Indigenous rhetorical practices to contemporary discussions about technology, Haas argues that what we position as "discoveries" or recent developments in rhetoric may actually erase (intentionally or not) long-standing cultural practices that have been taking place for centuries both in and outside our classrooms and workplaces. Elaborating on this argument, Haas continues by explaining that the word *digital* "refers to our fingers, our digits, one of the primary ways (along with our ears and eyes) through which we make sense of the world and with which we write into the world" (84).

My goal for this book was to illustrate the multilayered ways in which multilinguals make sense of the world as they are simultaneously impacted by the world—a world that inherently excludes the communicative and intellectual contributions of people who work outside the limitations of Western, English-dominant rhetorical frameworks. To be sure, the frameworks that I present in this book are not, as Haas cautions, new "discoveries." Although the stories of my participants serve as representations of why language diversity matters to contemporary discussions about writing research and practice, I encourage writing researchers, teachers, and professionals to further engage with the rhetorical work of translation, pushing this project further into analyses across different contexts, languages, and communities.

As we consider how to expand concepts like translation moments and A Revised Rhetoric of Translation, I also encourage us to think about the ways in which translation in itself can serve as a technology that can help us and our students continue repositioning writing beyond standardized written English. As a techne that facilitates creativity and craftsmanship, translation can help us continue recognizing and giving credit to the rhetorical, creative work of linguistic diversity, helping push against deficit models that, for many decades, have been geared toward linguistically diverse individuals in the United States. By recognizing translation as a powerful technology that is already embedded in the cultural practices of marginalized communities, we can better account for the intellectual labor of language translation that takes place both inside and outside our classrooms. Furthermore, in teaching translation as a technology (through concepts like translation moments and A Revised Rhetoric of Translation), we can continue to reposition language diversity at the center of our classroom and professional practices, rather than isolating language transformation work to something that only applies to some populations. In this way, we can "consider how our commitment to communities [and diversity] challenges [and informs] our disciplinary norms" (Ríos, "Cultivating," 63). By leveraging translation and all its multilingual/multimodal elements, we can also continue to focus on the many powerful contributions (rather than challenges) that language diversity offers us, our students, our communities, and our fields of study.

Notes

Introduction

1. Named languages are categories given to linguistic patterns, typically organized by nations or social groups. Examples of named languages include English, Spanish, and French. While named languages are often identified in the singular (i.e., we refer to "English" rather than "Englishes"), I here reference named languages while acknowledging the fluid nature of all communication, understanding that there are multiple and constantly changing "Englishes," "Spanishes," and so on (Otheguy, García, and Reid).

Chapter 1

1. *Plurinationalism* is defined as the coexistence of different nationalities within a larger state. Bolivia is made up of nine departments, each of which have legal independence. As a result, each department can establish its official language(s), and all the official languages are recognized as national languages in the country as a whole.

2. Although this chapter specifically cites scholarship in sociolinguistics, rhetoric and composition, and translation studies, my development of translation moments as analytical units for studying language fluidity is also influenced by fluid and decolonial approaches to language and communication proposed by scholars of African American language, Indigenous rhetorics (including Chicanx rhetorics), and Latinx rhetorics and by scholarship on social activism and civic engagement in rhetoric and composition, technical communication, and English Education. I expand on this work in my discussion of multimodality and method/ologies and in the presentation of data throughout this book.

3. The diagram in figure 3 is a representative illustration of a written translation workflow. In this project, I discuss both written translations and spoken translations (i.e., interpretation). Translation moments can be experienced in both written translation and interpretation sessions and encompass a pause that signals rhetorical negotiation on the part of the translator or interpreter. However, the data in this project does not always distinguish between written translation and verbal interpretation. Transla-

tors who participated in this project frequently spoke to other collaborators when completing written translations, and participating interpreters frequently wrote or sketched things to clarify meaning during verbal interpretation sessions.

Chapter 2

1. *Testimonios* are stories told to reflect and represent the historical experiences of marginalized people (Torrez, "Translating").

Chapter 3

1. Although I draw on the concept of "mestiza consciousness" as it is described by Anzaldúa, I acknowledge Gabriela Raquel Ríos's important critique about "the problematic ways many Chican@s and others have taken in advancing a Nahua form of indigenous rhetoric because we have done so using primarily a Western frame of reference and because we exercise a Mestizaje hegemony over other indigenous peoples in Cemanahuac (Latin America) when articulating a Chican@ or Mestizaje rhetorical tradition" ("Performing," 85). I also honor the important clarification by Eric Rodriguez and Everardo Cuevas, in "Problematizing *Mestizaje*," that "Mestizaje has been used to create a sense of nationalistic pride that is colonial in its erasure of Indigenous epistemologies and ontologies." While I find Anzaldúa's concepts of "mestiza consciousness" and *conocimiento* to be useful in bridging conversations about language and multimodality, I do not intend to suggest that all Chicanx lived experiences are homogenous, and I honor the multiple and overlapping Indigenous cultures and practices that often go unrecognized and unacknowledged in discussions of Chicanx identities. I am grateful to Indigenous and Chicanx scholars and students who continue to expand my uptake of decolonial method/ologies and orientations in and beyond this project.

References

Agboka, Godwin Y. "Participatory Localization: A Social Justice Approach to Navigating Unenfranchised/Disenfranchised Cultural Sites." *Technical Communication Quarterly* 22, no. 1 (2013): 28–49.

Alvarez, Steven. "Translanguaging Tareas: Emergent Bilingual Youth as Language Brokers for Homework in Immigrant Families." *Language Arts* 91, no. 5 (2014): 326.

Anzaldúa, Gloria E. "Now Let Us Shift . . . The Path of Conocimiento . . . Inner Work, Public Acts." In *This Bridge We Call Home: Radical Visions for Transformation*, edited by Gloria Anzaldúa and AnaLouise Keating, 540–78. Routledge, 2002.

Arce, Nicole. "Translation Tools Getting Better and Better: Google Ups the Ante with Translate Update." *Tech Times*, 18 Jan. 2015. http://www.techtimes.com/articles/27234/20150118/translation-tools-getting-better-and-better-google-ups-the-ante-with-translate-update.htm

Arola, Kristin, Cheryl E. Ball, and Jennifer Sheppard. "Multimodality as a Frame for Individual and Institutional Change." *Digital Pedagogy Lab*, 10 Jan. 2014. http://www.digitalpedagogylab.com/hybridped/multimodality-frame-individual-institutional-change/

Arola, Kristin L., and Anne Wysocki, eds. *Composing (Media) = Composing (Embodiment): Bodies, Technologies, Writing, the Teaching of Writing*. University Press of Colorado, 2012.

Baker, Mona. *Translation and Conflict: A Narrative Account*. Routledge, 2006.

Balk, Ethan M, Mei Chung, Nira Hadar, Kamal Patel, Winifred W. Yu, Thomas A. Trikalinos, and Lina Kong Win Chang. "Accuracy of Data Extraction of Non-English Language Trials with Google Translate." *Methods Research Report*, Apr. 2012. http://www.ncbi.nlm.nih.gov/books/NBK95238/

Ball, Cheryl E., Kristin Arola, and Jennifer Sheppard. *Writer/Designer: A Guide to Making Multimodal Projects*. Bedford / St. Martin's, 2014.

Banks, Adam. *Digital Griots: African American Rhetoric in a Multimedia Age*. Southern Illinois University Press, 2011.

Barton, David, and Carmen Lee. *Language Online: Investigating Digital Texts and Practices*. Routledge, 2013.

Batova, Tatiana, and Dave Clark. "The Complexities of Globalized Content Management." *Journal of Business and Technical Communication* 29, no. 2 (2015): 221–35.

Berry, Patrick W., Gail E. Hawisher, and Cynthia L. Selfe, eds. *Transnational Literate Lives in Digital Times*. Utah State University Press / Computers and Composition Digital Press, 2012.

Blommaert, Jan. *The Sociolinguistics of Globalization*. Cambridge University Press, 2010.

Bloom-Pojar, Rachel. *Translanguaging Outside the Academy: Negotiating Rhetoric and Healthcare in the Spanish Caribbean*. CCCC Studies in Writing and Rhetoric, 2018.

Blythe, Stuart, and Laura Gonzales. "Coordination and Transfer across the Metagenre of Secondary Research." *College Composition and Communication* 67, no. 4 (2016): 607–33.

Bowen, Tracey, and Carl Whithaus, eds. *Multimodal Literacies and Emerging Genres*. University of Pittsburgh Press, 2013.

Butler, Janine. "Where Access Meets Multimodality: The Case of ASL Music Videos." *Kairos: A Journal of Rhetoric, Technology, and Pedagogy* 21, no. 1 (2016). http://kairos.technorhetoric.net/21.1/topoi/butler/index.html

Brumberger, Eva R. "Visual Rhetoric in the Curriculum Pedagogy for a Multimodal Workplace." *Business Communication Quarterly* 68, no. 3 (2005): 318–33.

Byrne, Jody. *Technical Translation: Usability Strategies for Translating Technical Documentation*. Springer, 2006.

Canagarajah, A. Suresh. "Negotiating Translingual Literacy: An Enactment." *Research in the Teaching of English* 48, no. 1 (2013): 40–67.

Canagarajah, A. Suresh. "A Rhetoric of Shuttling between Languages." In *Cross-Language Relations in Composition*, edited by Bruce Horner, Min-Zhan Lu, and Paul Kei Matsuda, 158–79. Southern Illinois University Press, 2010.

Canagarajah, A. Suresh. *Translingual Practice: Global Englishes and Cosmopolitan Relations*. Routledge, 2013.

Chen, Jianping, and Yu Bao. "Cross-Language Search: The Case of Google Language Tools." *First Monday* 14, no. 3 (2009). http://firstmonday.org/article/view/2335/2116

Crystal, David. "The Internet: A Linguistic Revolution." Pari Center for New Learning. Accessed 26 April 2017. http://www.paricenter.com/library/papers/crystal01.php

Cronin, Michael. *Translation Goes to the Movies*. Routledge, 2008.

Dimitrova, Bergitta Englund. *Expertise and Explicitation in the Translation Process*. Benjamins Translation Library 64. John Benjamins, 2005.

ElShiekh, Ahmed Abdel Azim. "Google Translate Service: Transfer of Meaning, Distortion, or Simply a New Creation? An Investigation into the Translation Process and Problems at Google." *English Language and Literature Studies* 2, no. 1 (2012): 56–68.

Fraiberg, Steven. "Composition 2.0: Toward a Multilingual and Multimodal Framework." *College Composition and Communication* 62, no. 1 (2010): 100–126.

Frost, Alanna, and Suzanne Blum Malley. *Multilingual Literacy Landscapes: A Curated*

Exhibit from the Digital Archive of Literacy Narratives. Computers and Composition Digital Press, 2012. http://ccdigitalpress.org/stories/chapters/frost/

García, Ofelia. *Bilingual Education in the 21st Century: A Global Perspective.* Wiley, 2011.

García, Ofelia, Nelson Flores, and Heather Homonoff Woodley. "Constructing In-Between Spaces to 'Do' Bilingualism: A Tale of Two High Schools in One City." In *Multilingual Education: Between Language Learning and Translanguaging*, edited by Jasone Cenoz and Durk Gorter, 199–224. Cambridge University Press, 2015.

García, Ofelia, and Li Wei. *Translanguaging: Language, Bilingualism, and Education.* Palgrave Macmillan, 2014.

Gilyard, Keith. "The Rhetoric of Translingualism." *College English* 78, no. 3 (2016): 284–89.

Gnecchi, Marusca, Bruce Maylath, Birthe Mousten, and Sonia Vandepitte. "Field Convergence: Merging Roles of Technical Writers and Technical Translators." *IEEE Transactions on Professional Communication* 54 (2011): 168–84.

Grabill, Jeffrey T. *Writing Community Change: Designing Technologies for Citizen Action.* Hampton Press, 2007.

Gonzales, Laura. "But Is That Relevant *Here*? A Pedagogical Model for Embedding Translation Training within Technical Communication Courses in the US." *Connexions: International Professional Communication Journal* 5, no. 1 (2017). https://connexionsj.files.wordpress.com/2017/06/gonzales2.pdf

Gonzales, Laura. "Multimodality, Translingualism, and Rhetorical Genre Studies." *Composition Forum* 31 (2015). http://compositionforum.com/issue/31/multimodality.php

Gonzales, Laura. "Sites of Translation: What Multilinguals Can Teach Us about Writing, Rhetoric, and Technology." PhD diss., Michigan State University, 2016.

Gonzales, Laura. "Using ELAN Video Coding Software to Analyze the Rhetorics of Translation." *Kairos: A Journal of Rhetoric, Technology, and Pedagogy* 21, no. 2 (2017). http://praxis.technorhetoric.net/tiki-index.php?page=PraxisWiki:_:ELAN

Gonzales, Laura, and Heather Noel Turner. "Converging Fields, Expanding Outcomes: Technical Communication, Translation, and Design at a Non-Profit Organization." *Technical Communication* 64, no. 2 (2017): 126–40.

Gonzales, Laura, and Rebecca Zantjer. "Translation as a User-Localization Practice." *Technical Communication* 62, no. 4 (2015): 271–84.

Guerra, Juan C. "Cultivating a Rhetorical Sensibility in the Translingual Writing Classroom." *College English* 78, no. 3 (2016): 228–33.

Guerra, Juan C. *Language, Culture, Identity and Citizenship in College Classrooms and Communities.* Routledge, 2015.

Gumperz, John J., and Edward Hernandez. "Cognitive Aspects of Bilingual Communication." Working Papers of the Language-Behavior Research Laboratory 28, University of California, Berkeley, 1969.

Haas, Angela M. "Race, Rhetoric, and Technology: A Case Study of Decolonial Technical Communication Theory, Methodology, and Pedagogy." *Journal of Business and Technical Communication* 26, no. 3 (2012): 277–310.

Haas, Angela M. "Toward a Decolonial Digital and Visual American Indian Rhetorics Pedagogy." In *Survivance, Sovereignty, and Story: Teaching American Indian Rhetorics*, edited by Lisa King, Rose Gubele, and Joyce Rain Anderson, 188–208. Utah State University Press, 2015.

Haas, Angela M. "Wampum as Hypertext: An American Indian Intellectual Tradition of Multimedia Theory and Practice." *Studies in American Indian Literatures* 19, no. 4 (2007): 77–100.

Hawisher, Gail E., and Cynthia L. Selfe. "Globalism and Multimodality in a Digitized World." *Pedagogy: Critical Approaches to Teaching Literature, Language, Composition, and Culture* 10, no. 1 (2009): 55–68.

Hawisher, Gail E., Cynthia L. Selfe, Patrick W. Berry, and Synne Skjulstad. "Conclusion: Closing Thoughts on Research Methodology." In *Transnational Literate Lives in Digital Times*, edited by Patrick Barry, Gail E. Hawisher, and Cynthia L. Selfe. Computers and Composition Digital Press / Utah State University Press, 2012. Accessed 1 Dec. 2013. http://ccdigitalpress.org/transnational/conclusion1.html

Heath, Shirley Brice. "Ever-Shifting Oral and Literate Traditions." In *Perspectives on Literacy*, edited by Eugene R. Kintgen, Barry M. Kroll, and Mike Rose, 348–70. Southern Illinois University Press, 1988.

Hirvonen, Maija, and Liisa Tiittula. "A Method for Analysing Multimodal Research Material: Audio Description in Focus." *Electronic Proceedings of the KäTu Symposium on Translation and Interpreting Studies* 4 (2010). http://studyres.com/doc/22468607/a-method-for-analysing-multimodal-research-material--audio

Horner, Bruce, Min-Zhan Lu, Jacqueline Jones Royster, and John Trimbur. "Language Difference in Writing: Toward a Translingual Approach." *College English* 73, no. 3 (2011): 303–21.

Horner, Bruce, Cynthia Selfe, and Tim Lockridge. "Translinguality, Transmodality, and Difference: Exploring Dispositions and Change in Language and Learning." *Enculturation Intermezzo* 1 (2015). http://intermezzo.enculturation.net/01/ttd-horner-selfe-lockridge/index.htm

Jacquemond, Richard. "Translation and Cultural Hegemony: The Case of French–Arabic Translation." In *Rethinking Translation: Discourse, Subjectivity, Ideology*, edited by Lawrence Venuti, 139–58. Routledge, 1992.

Jiménez, Robert T., Sam David, Keenan Fagan, Victoria J. Risko, Mark Pacheco, Lisa Pray, and Mark Gonzales. "Using Translation to Drive Conceptual Development for Students Becoming Literate in English as an Additional Language." *Research in the Teaching of English* 49, no. 3 (2015): 248–71.

Jordan, Jay. "Redesigning Composition for Multilingual Realities." Paper presented at the Conference on College Composition and Communication of the National Council of Teachers of English, St. Louis, MO, 23 Mar. 2012.

Kells, Michelle Hall. "Writing Across Communities: Deliberation and the Discursive Possibilities of WAC." *Reflections* 11, no. 1 (2007): 87–108.

Ketola, Anne. "Towards a Multimodally Oriented Theory of Translation: A Cognitive Framework for the Translation of Illustrated Technical Texts." *Translation Studies* 9, no. 1 (2015): 67–81.

Khubchandani, Lachman M. "A Plurilingual Ethos: A Peep into the Sociology of Language." *Indian Journal of Applied Linguistics* 24, no. 1 (1998): 5–37.

Kramsch, Claire J. *The Multilingual Subject: What Foreign Language Learners Say about Their Experience and Why It Matters.* Oxford University Press, 2009.

Kress, Gunther. *Multimodality: A Social Semiotic Approach to Contemporary Communication*. Routledge, 2010.

Kress, Gunther. "What Is a Mode?" Video, uploaded by Jeff Bezemer, 9:17, 15 Mar. 2012. https://www.youtube.com/watch?v=kJ2gz_OQHhI

Leon, Kendall. "Chicanas Making Change: Institutional Rhetoric and the Comisión Femenil Mexicana Nacional." *Reflections* 13, no. 1 (2013): 165–94.

Lorimer Leonard, Rebecca. "Multilingual Writing as Rhetorical Attunement." *College English* 76, no. 3 (2014): 227–47.

Lu, Min-Zhan, and Bruce Horner. "Introduction: Translingual Work." *College English* 78, no. 3 (2016): 207–18.

Lu, Min-Zhan, and Bruce Horner. "Translingual Literacy, Language Difference, and Matters of Agency." *College English* 75, no. 6 (2013): 582–607.

Lyons, Erin. "How Information Technology Developments are Changing the Future of Medical Translation." *ATA Chronicle* 42, no. 1 (2013). http://www.atanet.org/chronicle-online/wpcontent/uploads/4201_19_erin_lyons.pdf

Makoni, Sinfree, and Alastair Pennycook. "Disinventing and (Re)Constituting Languages." *Critical Inquiry in Language Studies: An International Journal* 2, no. 3 (2005): 137–56.

Makoni, Sinfree, and Alastair Pennycook, eds. *Disinventing and Reconstituting Languages*. Clevedon, UK: Multilingual Matters, 2007.

Matsuda, Paul Kei. "The Lure of Translingual Writing." *PMLA* 129, no. 3 (2014): 478–83.

Maylath, Bruce, Ricardo Muñoz Martín, and Marta Pacheco Pinto. "Translation and International Professional Communication: Building Bridges and Strengthening Skills." *Connexions: International Professional Communication Journal* 3, no. 2 (2015): 3–9.

McKee, Heidi A., and Danielle Nicole DeVoss, eds. *Digital Writing Research: Technologies, Methodologies, and Ethical Issues*. Hampton Press, 2007.

McNeill, David. "Gesture and Language Dialectic." *Acta Linguistica Hafniensia* 34, no. 1 (2002): 7–37.

Milson-Whyte, Vivette. "Pedagogical and Socio-Political Implications of Code-Meshing in Classrooms: Some Considerations for Translingual Orientation to Writing." In *Literacy as a Translingual Practice: Between Communities and Classrooms*, edited by A. Suresh Canagarajah, 115–27. Routledge, 2013.

Monberg, Terese Guinsatao. "Writing Home or Writing as Community: Toward a Theory of Recursive Spatial Movement for Students of Color in Service-Learning Courses." *Reflections* 8, no. 3 (2009): 21–51.

Moraga, Cherríe, and Gloria Anzaldúa, eds. *This Bridge Called My Back: Writings by Radical Women of Color*. SUNY Press, 2015.

Müller, Martin. What's in a Word? Problematizing Translation between Languages. *Area* 39, no. 2 (2007): 206–13.

National Council of Teachers of English. "The NCTE Definition of 21st Century Literacies." NCTE, 2013. Accessed 3 Apr. 2016. http://www.ncte.org/positions/statements/21stcentdefinition

New London Group. "A Pedagogy of Multiliteracies: Designing Social Futures." *Harvard Educational Review* 66, no. 1 (1996): 60–92.

Newmark, Peter. *A Textbook of Translation*. Prentice Hall, 1988.

Otheguy, Ricardo, Ofelia García, and Wallis Reid. "Clarifying Translanguaging and Deconstructing Named Languages: A Perspective from Linguistics." *Applied Linguistics Review* 6, no. 3 (2015): 281–307.

Pennycook, Alastair. "English as a Language Always in Translation." *European Journal of English Studies* 12, no. 1 (2008): 33–47.

Pigg, Stacey. "Emplacing Mobile Composing Habits: A Study of Academic Writing in Networked Social Spaces." *College Composition and Communication* 66, no. 2 (2014): 250–75.

Pym, Anthony. "Redesigning Translation Competence in an Electronic Age: In Defense of a Minimalist Approach." *Meta: Translators' Journal* 48, no. 4 (2003): 481–97.

Redden, Elizabeth. "International Student Numbers Top 1 Million." *Inside Higher Ed,* 14 Nov. 2016. https://www.insidehighered.com/news/2016/11/14/annual-open-doors-report-documents-continued-growth-international-students-us-and-us

Ríos, Gabriela Raquel. "Cultivating Land-Based Literacies and Rhetorics." *Literacy in Composition Studies* 3, no. 1 (2015): 60–70.

Ríos, Gabriela Raquel. "Performing Nahua Rhetorics for Civic Engagement." In *Survivance, Sovereignty, and Story: Teaching American Indian Rhetorics,* edited by Lisa King, Rose Gubele, and Joyce Rain Anderson, 79–95. Utah State University Press, 2015.

Robinson, Douglas. *Translation and Empire.* St. Jerome Publishing, 1997.

Rodriguez, Eric, and Everardo J. Cuevas. "Problematizing *Mestizaje.*" *Composition Studies* 45, no. 2 (2017).

Saldaña, Johnny. *The Coding Manual for Qualitative Researchers.* 2nd ed. Sage, 2015.

Sánchez, Raúl. "Outside the Text: Retheorizing Empiricism and Identity." *College English* 74, no. 3 (2012): 234–46.

Selfe, Cynthia L., ed. *Multimodal Composition Resources for Teachers.* Hampton Press, 2007.

Selfe, Cynthia L., and Bruce Horner. "Translinguality/Transmodality Relations: Snapshots from a Dialogue." Working Papers Series on Negotiating Differences in Language and Literacy, University of Louisville, 2013. Accessed 5 July 2014. https://louisville.edu/workingpapers/doc/self-horner-working-papers-version

Seloni, Lisya. "Academic Literacy Socialization of First Year Doctoral Students in US: A Micro-Ethnographic Perspective." *English for Specific Purposes* 31, no. 7 (2012): 47–59.

Seloni, Lisya. "'I'm an Artist and a Scholar Who Is Trying to Find a Middle Point': A Textographic Analysis of a Colombian Art Historian's Thesis Writing." *Journal of Second Language Writing* 25 (2014): 79–99.

Shipka, Jody. "Including, but Not Limited to, the Digital: Composing Multimodal Texts." In *Multimodal Literacies and Emerging Genres,* edited by Tracey Bowen and Carl Whithaus, 73–90. University of Pittsburgh Press, 2013.

Shipka, Jody. *Toward a Composition Made Whole.* University of Pittsburgh Press, 2011.

Shipka, Jody. "Transmodality in/and Processes of Making: Changing Dispositions and Practice." *College English* 78, no. 3 (2016): 250–57.

Shivers-McNair, Ann. "3D Interviewing with Researcher POV Video: Bodies and Knowledge in the Making." *Kairos: A Journal of Rhetoric, Technology, and Pedagogy* 21, no. 2 (2017). http://praxis.technorhetoric.net/tiki-index. php?page=PraxisWiki:_:3D%20Interviewing

Slattery, Shaun. "Un-Distributing Work through Writing: How Technical Writers Manage Texts in Complex Information Environments." *Technical Communication Quarterly* 16, no. 3 (2007): 311–25.

Smitherman, Geneva. *Talkin and Testifyin: The Language of Black America.* 1977; rpt., Wayne State University Press, 1986.

Smitherman, Geneva, and Victor Villanueva. *Language Diversity in the Classroom: From Intention to Practice.* Southern Illinois University Press, 2003.

Sun, Huatong. *Cross-Cultural Technology Design: Creating Culture-Sensitive Technology for Local Users.* Oxford University Press, 2012.

Takayoshi, Pamela, and Cynthia L. Selfe. "Thinking about Multimodality." In *Multimodal Composition: Resources for Teachers,* edited by Cynthia L. Selfe, 1–12. Hampton Press, 2007.

Torrez, J. Estrella. "Somos Mexicanos y Hablamos Mexicano Aqui: Rural Farmworker Families' Struggles to Maintain Cultural and Linguistic Identity in Michigan." *Journal of Language, Identity, and Education* 12, no. 4 (2013): 277–94.

Torrez, J. Estrella. "Translating Chicana Testimonios into Pedagogy for a White Midwestern Classroom." *Chicana/Latina Studies: The Journal of Mujeres Activas en Letras y Cambio Social* 14, no. 2 (2015): 100–130.

Tymoczko, Maria. *Enlarging Translation, Empowering Translators.* St. Jerome Publishing, 2007.

Tymoczko, Maria. "Ideology and the Position of the Translator: In What Sense Is a Translator 'In Between'?" In *Apropos of Ideology: Translation Studies on Ideology—Ideologies in Translation Studies,* edited by Maria Caldeza-Pérez, 181–201. St. Jerome Publishing, 2003.

Tymoczko, Maria. "Translation and Political Engagement: Activism, Social Change, and the Role of Translation in Geopolitical Shifts." *Translator* 6, no. 1 (2000): 23–47.

Vigouroux, Cécile B., and Salikoko S. Mufwene, eds. *Globalization and Language Vitality: Perspectives from Africa.* Bloomsbury Academic, 2008.

Walton, Rebecca, M. Zraly, and J. P. Mugengana. "Values and Validity: Navigating Messiness in a Community-Based Research Project in Rwanda." *Technical Communication Quarterly* 24, no. 1 (2015): 45–69.

Wei, Li. "Moment Analysis and Translanguaging Space: Discursive Construction of Identities by Multilingual Chinese Youth in Britain." *Journal of Pragmatics* 43, no. 5 (2011): 1222–35.

Williams, Miriam, and Octavio Pimentel, eds. *Communicating Race, Ethnicity, and Identity in Technical Communication.* Routledge, 2016.

Wolfram, Walt. "The Relationship of White Southern Speech to Vernacular Black English." *Language* 50, no. 3 (1974): 498–527.

Yajima, Yusaku, and Satoshi Toyosaki. "Bridging for a Critical Turn in Translation Studies: Power, Hegemony, and Empowerment." *Connexions: International Professional Communication Journal* 3, no. 2 (2016): 91–125.

Yancey, Kathleen Blake. "Made Not Only in Words: Composition in a New Key." *College Composition and Communication* 56, no. 2 (2004): 297–328.
Young, Vershawn A., and Aja Martinez. *Code Meshing as World English: Policy, Pedagogy, Performance.* National Council of Teachers of English, 2011.

Index

Printed and bound by CPI Group (UK) Ltd, Croydon, CR0 4YY

09/06/2025

14685674-0002